MARVEL STUDIOS

IRON MAN 2

CONTENTS

BASICS

Before you begin your adventure as Iron Man and War Machine, take some time to familiarize yourself with the game's controls and menus.

HEADQUARTERS

Manage your suit, weapons and equipment before departing on a mission. Use the Left Stick or D-Pad to select a category or menu item, and press the A or X button to make a selection. Press the B or Circle button to cancel or return to the previous menu.

MISSIONS

JARVIS shows a summary of the current suit you have selected, its loadout, and an image that displays which mission you have selected currently. Press the X or Square button to change the suit selection, the Y or Triangle Button to change the mission selection, or the Left Bumper or L1 to toggle between the last customized Iron Man armor and War Machine armor.

Note that JARVIS keeps a record of every mission Tony attempts. Completed missions can be reattempted in a simulation, and you can also select the next mission to advance the story.

FIELD DATA

After completing a mission, you earn Field Data based on how well you performed. Defeating more enemies and avoiding damage to the hero's armor increase the Field Data that is earned.

This Field Data is used in Research to invent ammunition, weapon upgrades, weapon modules, and close combat program upgrades.

SUIT CUSTOMIZATION

At the Headquarters, choose a suit to wear and outfit it the way you see fit.

Suit Selection

Select a suit. Not all suits are available at all times. Some suits become available when enough Field Data has been collected through mission completion with numerous enemies defeated and armor integrity minimally compromised.

Weapons Loadout

Choose what to install in each available position of the suit. Use Up and Down to toggle the active slot, and press the A or X button to select a weapon to equip. Not all weapons can be equipped to all slots.

Close Combat Programs

Each suit can be loaded with two Close Combat Programs. Use Up and Down to toggle the active slot, and press the A or X button to select a combat program to load.

FABRICATION

Once weapons have been upgraded, and ammunition and modules have been invented, they can be assembled into a custom weapon for your armor suits. Use Up and Down to toggle the active slot, and press the A or X button to select an item to install from those you have invented.

RESEARCH

Using Field Data gathered on missions, Tony can invent new weapons, ammunition, or modules for his suit. Development requires a certain amount of field data which is indicated on the left of the screen for each item. If you have sufficient field data, then selecting the item completes the invention.

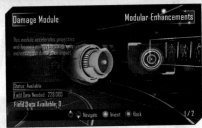

Weapons Development

Select a weapon to upgrade it to an improved version. Weapons begin at Mark I, and can be upgraded up to Mark III.

Modular Enhancements

Select a module to invent. These can be fitted to Mark I, II and III weapons to customize their performance.

Ammunition Invention

Select an ammunition type to invent. These can be loaded into Mark I, II and III weapons to improve their battlefield effectiveness.

Close Combat Programs

Select a combat routine to improve and update.

MORE DETAILS AVAILABLE

For more information about Weapons Development, Modular Enhancements, Ammunition, and Close Combat Programs, flip ahead to the Customization chapter.

HEAD-UP DISPLAY

1. *Left Weapon*
2. *Right Weapon*
3. *Power Routing*
4. *Shield Status*

5. *Armor Integrity*
6. *Current Combat Program*
7. *Current Objective*
8. *Radar*

CONTROLS

XBOX 360

The default control scheme during gameplay is as follows:

	ENVIRONMENT	IN FLIGHT
LEFT STICK	Move character	
RIGHT STICK	Move camera/target reticule/targeting box in all directions	
Y BUTTON	Ascend (hover)	Increase altitude
A BUTTON	Descend, land	Decrease altitude
X BUTTON	Melee attack	
B BUTTON	Break enemy's attack chain, grapple vulnerable enemy	
LEFT ON D-PAD	Switch left weapon	
RIGHT ON D-PAD	Switch right weapon	
UP ON D-PAD	Select melee attack combat program	
DOWN ON D-PAD	Hold to use Special Ability	
LEFT BUMPER	Engage afterburners, double tap to enter full flight mode	
RIGHT BUMPER	Lock on, use the right stick to change locked-on target	
LEFT TRIGGER	Fire secondary weapon	
RIGHT TRIGGER	Fire primary weapon	
START BUTTON	Pause and display Pause menu	

PLAYSTATION 3

The default control scheme during gameplay is as follows:

	GROUND ENVIRONMENT	IN FLIGHT
LEFT STICK	Move character	
RIGHT STICK	Move camera/target reticule/targeting box in all directions	
TRIANGLE BUTTON	Ascend (hover)	Increase altitude
X BUTTON	Descend, land	Decrease altitude
SQUARE BUTTON	Melee attack	
CIRCLE BUTTON	Break enemy's attack chain, grapple vulnerable enemy	
LEFT ON D-PAD	Switch left weapon	
RIGHT ON D-PAD	Switch right weapon	
UP ON D-PAD	Select melee attack combat program	
DOWN ON D-PAD	Hold to use Special Ability	
L1	Engage afterburners, double tap to enter full flight mode	
R1	Lock on, use the right stick to change locked-on target	
L2	Fire secondary weapon	
R2	Fire primary weapon	
START BUTTON	Pause and display Pause menu	

MOVEMENT

Use the Left Stick to guide Iron Man's motion depending on the situation:

When your hero is walking on the ground, use the Left Stick to run in any direction.

When your hero is hovering, use the Left Stick to hover in each direction. You can adjust his altitude with the Ascend and Descend buttons.

When in Flight mode, use the Left Stick to move left or right.

TARGETING

Press RB or R1 to toggle the lock-on. When toggled on, you lock onto the closest enemy to the targeting reticule. The reticule turns red when locked-on. Also, while locked on, use the Right Stick to switch to another enemy in sight. Press RB or R1 to disengage lock-on mode and return to manual aiming.

HOVERING

Press the Y or Triangle button to hover in mid-air. Hovering is the ideal position for examining the environment, or when attacking both ground and aerial forces.

Hold the Y or Triangle button to ascend further into the air. Hold the A or X button to descend back to the ground.

FLIGHT

Push the left bumper once to engage afterburners for a short boost of speed, or twice to enter full flight mode. In full flight mode, press Up to increase speed, Down to brake, and Left and Right to strafe to each side. Use the right stick to control your direction of flight.

Your hero can perform a Barrel Roll in flight by holding LB or L1 and pressing Left or Right. Press Down while holding LB or L1 to perform a 180 turn.

DODGE

Tap LB or L1 for a burst of speed in the direction you are moving. This can be used on the ground or in flight and is very important in avoiding much of the enemy weapon fire.

POWER ROUTING

The bars on the left hand side of the screen indicate the current state of how the suit is routing power to the three primary systems; the thrusters, shields and weapons respectively. The settings are dictated by whether you are on the ground, hovering in the air, or in full flight mode.

GROUND Being on the ground means your shields and weapons get full power. This means your shields regenerate at an increased rate and your ammunition replenishes faster.

HOVER While hovering, your thrusters are allocated power to maintain altitude, so your shields and weapons regenerate at a lowered rate.

FULL FLIGHT During full flight mode, your thrusters are allocated full power to achieve maximum speed, but your shields are sacrificed and ammunition replenishment is reduced to a minimum.

INTERACTION COMMANDS

On approaching an object that can be interacted with, such as a control panel, a button icon is displayed on screen. Press the button displayed to interact with the object. In some cases the button may need to be pressed repeatedly. You can also interact with some enemies, allowing very powerful special attacks.

SUIT'S DEFENSES

Your suit's defenses are shown in the lower left of the screen. The outer band shows shielding, which regenerates over time. The inner ring shows armor integrity, which does not recover.

MELEE

Tap the X or Square button to engage in melee combat. During melee, use the Left Stick to control the direction of your next strike.

Press the B or Circle button when you see your hero blocking to break an enemy's combo. Also, if you stun an enemy, use the B or Circle button to take it out of the fight: Iron Man can reprogram some enemies to fight for you, and War Machine can drive them berserk.

GRAPPLE

When close to a vulnerable opponent, as indicated by a button icon, press the B or Circle button to grapple it. This can result in disabling, destroying, or even temporarily converting the enemy to your side.

When you have been grappled by an enemy, you can fight free by following the on-screen prompts.

CLOSE COMBAT PROGRAMS

Each Close Combat program has a specialty: stun, damage, or area effects. Both heroes have a program that corresponds with each of these specialties. You can have two in your suit loadout. Switch between them by pressing Up on the D-Pad.

This determines the combat routine that will be engaged during melee attacks.

All close combat programs have a core combination of moves: X, X, X, X or Square, Square, Square, Square.

When you see the gold trail on a move, that's the final blow of the combo. On the final blow, you can trigger a finishing move by pressing B or Circle.

Close combat programs can be upgraded in Research. Advanced and Ultimate versions have additional moves. Advanced Close Combat Programs have power moves that can end a chain of attacks by holding X or Square instead of tapping it. Ultimate versions of close combat programs have a second combo: X, B, X, X, X, X or Square, Circle, Square, Square, Square, Square.

SPECIAL ABILITY

Both heroes have a special ability that can be used by holding Down on the D-Pad. Iron Man's ability is Invincibility. Use this to avoid taking damage for

a short while. War Machine's ability is Omega System. Use this to power up his weapons for a short while.

GROUND POUND

Double tap the A or X button while hovering to pound the ground, which damages anything nearby.

MISSILE DEFLECTION

Iron Man and War Machine have the ability to deflect an enemy's missiles. A warning sound goes off when a homing missile is heading toward your hero, then a button icon appears to let you know that the missile can be deflected. Press the indicated button to deflect the missile back at whatever you are targeting.

BASICS

WEAPONRY

Iron Man and War Machine are both able to equip four different weapons. Two weapons are assigned to Left Trigger or L2 and the other two are assigned to Right Trigger or R2. Press Left on the D-pad to switch which weapon is fired on the left. Press Right to switch which weapon is fired on the right.

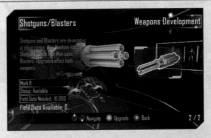

Repulsor

An Iron Man-only weapon, this palm-mounted energy emitter fires a pulse that can stagger enemies if the player holds the trigger down and charges it up before firing. It never runs out of ammunition or overheats.

Minigun

A War Machine-only weapon, this rotary cannon has nearly unlimited ammunition but can overheat. It recovers progressively while not being fired.

Blaster

An Iron Man-only weapon, this energy emitter functions similarly to a shotgun, doing great damage up close but scattering widely over range.

Shotgun

A War Machine-only weapon, this gun does great damage up close but scatters widely over range.

Laser

An Iron Man-only weapon, this high-powered beam fires as long as the trigger is held until its capacitor runs dry. The capacitor charges up while the weapon is not firing.

Missile Launcher

Both heroes carry a version of this weapon. Holding down the trigger causes it to lock on to multiple targets, and releasing fires the missiles.

Rocket Launcher

Both heroes carry a version of this explosive weapon. It is unguided but does tremendous damage with its single round. Best used on slower or stationary targets.

Unibeam

An Iron Man-only weapon, this chest-mounted beam is used by holding Right Trigger + Left Trigger or R2 + L2 and charging it up before firing. It can do tremendous damage, and never runs out of ammunition nor overheats.

TONY STARK

The man in the Iron Man suit. He is a scientific genius, impossibly rich, and makes frequent wisecracks.

IRON MAN

Tony Stark's alter ego. While suited up as Iron Man, he can hover, fly, has weapons concealed throughout, and can fire repulsors from the palms of the hands. In this game, you start with the Mark IV Iron Man suit. As the game progresses, you unlock other suits by fulfilling certain criteria.

CHARACTERS

JARVIS

Tony Stark's AI. Helps him operate his suit; also helps Rhodey operate his.

JAMES "RHODEY" RHODES

A U.S. Air Force Colonel and a friend to Tony Stark. Rhodey pilots the War Machine suit. He is soft-spoken, professional, and responsible.

WAR MACHINE

The former Mark II Iron Man suit, adapted by Hammer Industries and the U.S. military so that it now has heavier armor and multiple external weapons.

CHARACTERS

PEPPER POTTS

Pepper is Tony's right-hand woman and CEO of Stark Industries.

S.H.I.E.L.D.

When the world's most state-of-the-art technology and best-trained soldiers just aren't enough, the Strategic Homeland Intervention, Enforcement and Logistics Division often calls upon Iron Man and War Machine to assist in their defense initiatives.

COMBAT AIR SUPPORT (TRANSPORT)

A modified helicopter with VTOL attitude jets that give it extra lifing power and stability when hovering. Armed with multiple weapons and capable of delivering S.H.I.E.L.D. troops or vehicles to a battle. Sometimes called a "Cassie" (from its acronym C.A.S.).

NICK FURY

The director of S.H.I.E.L.D. and commander of the Helicarrier.

NATASHA ROMANOV

An agent of S.H.I.E.L.D. assigned to keep an eye on Tony Stark.

HELICARRIER

S.H.I.E.L.D.'s airborne base of operations rivals Tony Stark's Iron Man armor as one of the most impressive pieces of technology ever created

A.I.M. [ADVANCED IDEA MECHANICS]

An unscrupulous global technology company run by Kearson DeWitt. Much of the inventions are built on stolen Stark technology.

ULTIMO

A rogue AI built from stolen JARVIS code. Appears in a skyscraper-tall battle chassis.

KEARSON DEWITT

Former Stark employee and scientist with a desire to destroy Tony Stark.

ROXXON

Multinational Industrial giant involved in energy production and military contracting. After purchasing Hammer Industries, they now operate the drone program for the U.S. military (though now they also sell to all comers, including General Shatalov).

RUSSIA

Russian separatists under command of General Shatalov.

CRIMSON DYNAMO

20-foot-tall power armor suit built by AIM for General Shatalov in exchange for the use of his Tesla power facility to power the processor farm needed to boot up ULTIMO.

GENERAL VALENTIN SHATALOV

Russian separatist leader and pilot of the Crimson Dynamo.

ENEMIES

Iron Man and War Machine face off against all types of enemies, from the human infantry of General Shatalov's Russian Separatists to giant, humanoid machines designed to destroy anything in their path.

RUSSIAN SEPARATISTS

Russian Separatist forces are encountered only in Missions 2 and 3. They pose little threat on their own, but can make things miserable if they're not eliminated quickly enough.

SOLDIERS

The soldiers are not much of a threat, but hit at least one with Iron Man's Unibeam to score the Unnecessary Force Achievement.

SPECIAL ABILITY		
None		

	HEALTH	
DAMAGE	MAIN ATTACK RANGED WEAPON	
	SECONDARY ATTACK NONE	

VEHICLES (TURRETS, TANKS, HELICOPTERS)

While slightly more resilient than the infantry, even the best weapons the Separatists have at their disposal won't stand up to Iron Man and War Machine for long.

SPECIAL ABILITY		
None		

	HEALTH	
DAMAGE	MAIN ATTACK RANGED WEAPON	
	SECONDARY ATTACK NONE	

ROXXON

Roxxon sells military equipment to anyone with sufficient resources, and in this case the buyer is General Shatalov's Russian Separatist movement. Roxxon's hardware is put to use by the Russians in Missions 1, 2, and 3.

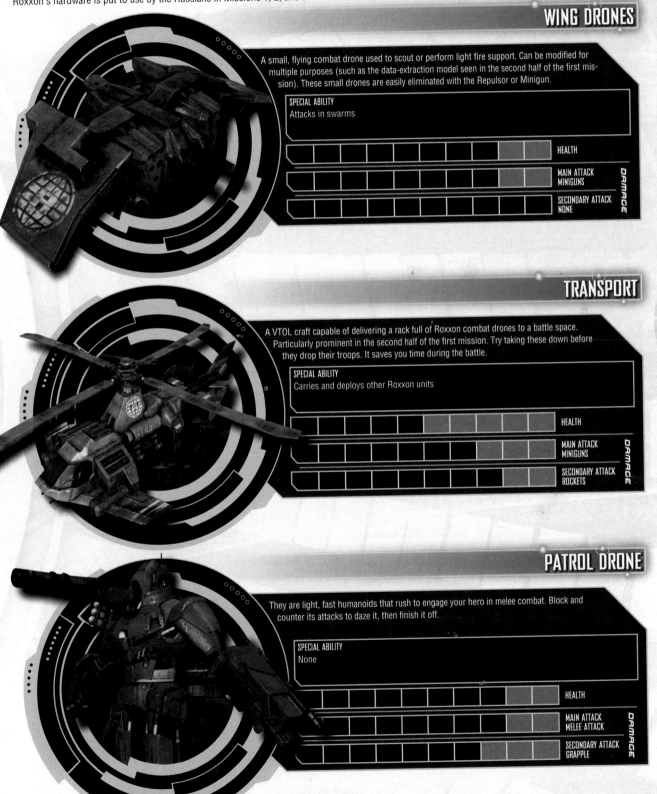

WING DRONES

A small, flying combat drone used to scout or perform light fire support. Can be modified for multiple purposes (such as the data-extraction model seen in the second half of the first mission). These small drones are easily eliminated with the Repulsor or Minigun.

SPECIAL ABILITY
Attacks in swarms

	HEALTH
MAIN ATTACK MINIGUNS	DAMAGE
SECONDARY ATTACK NONE	

TRANSPORT

A VTOL craft capable of delivering a rack full of Roxxon combat drones to a battle space. Particularly prominent in the second half of the first mission. Try taking these down before they drop their troops. It saves you time during the battle.

SPECIAL ABILITY
Carries and deploys other Roxxon units

	HEALTH
MAIN ATTACK MINIGUNS	DAMAGE
SECONDARY ATTACK ROCKETS	

PATROL DRONE

They are light, fast humanoids that rush to engage your hero in melee combat. Block and counter its attacks to daze it, then finish it off.

SPECIAL ABILITY
None

	HEALTH
MAIN ATTACK MELEE ATTACK	DAMAGE
SECONDARY ATTACK GRAPPLE	

ENEMIES

GRAPPLER DRONE

Large, well-armored humanoids that use ranged weapons and are also able to grapple your hero to pull him in close for melee combat. Deflect its missiles either back at the Grappler Drone or use them on another enemy. These units are often easily hijacked.

SPECIAL ABILITY
Employs a grapple claw to pull targets into melee range

	HEALTH										

| DAMAGE | MAIN ATTACK GATLING GUN | | | | | | | | | | |
| | SECONDARY ATTACK MELEE SMASH | | | | | | | | | | |

ARMIGER

An enormous, four-legged fighting machine built for use by Roxxon's military clients, including General Shatalov. These are first encountered in Mission 2. Dodge its different attacks and pound it with rockets and missiles. Once vulnerable, finish it off with a final blow.

SPECIAL ABILITY
When damaged, the Armiger deploys turrets with a variety of attacks; additionally, if a target is on the ground the Armiger is capable of stomping it

	HEALTH										

| DAMAGE | MAIN ATTACK MAIN GUN | | | | | | | | | | |
| | SECONDARY ATTACK MISSILE BARRAGE | | | | | | | | | | |

BATTERY

They fire volleys of homing missiles and have hover capability. These units are rare and tough to take down. Use their missiles against them and bombard them with heavy weaponry.

SPECIAL ABILITY
None

	HEALTH										

| DAMAGE | MAIN ATTACK RANGED WEAPON | | | | | | | | | | |
| | SECONDARY ATTACK NONE | | | | | | | | | | |

A.I.M.

Advanced Idea Mechanics, under the direction of Kearson DeWitt, provides the majority of foes faced during Missions 4 through 7.

AIM WASP

A small, hovering combat drone used to support or defend other units. These are first found in mission 4 defending the vertical entry shaft. These are easily taken down with the Minigun or Repulsor.

SPECIAL ABILITY
Attacks in swarms

HEALTH

MAIN ATTACK
BEAM ATTACK

SECONDARY ATTACK
NONE

DAMAGE

AIM TRANSPORT

A multi-function hover-capable combat craft that can fight as a combat unit as well as deliver AIM drones to the battle. Try taking these down before they drop their troops—saving you time in battle.

SPECIAL ABILITY
Carries and deploys other AIM units

HEALTH

MAIN ATTACK
MINI GUNS

SECONDARY ATTACK
NONE

DAMAGE

PATROL DRONE

They are light, fast humanoids that rush to engage your hero with melee attacks. Block and counter its attacks to daze it, then finish it off.

SPECIAL ABILITY
None

HEALTH

MAIN ATTACK
MELEE ATTACK

SECONDARY ATTACK
GRAPPLE

DAMAGE

ENEMIES

GRAPPLER DRONE

Grappler Drones are large, well-armored humanoids that fire ranged weapons and can pull your hero in close for melee attacks. They are equipped with a flare that attracts homing missiles fired at it. These units are often easily hijacked.

SPECIAL ABILITY
Flare to disperse rockets

HEALTH											
DAMAGE — MAIN ATTACK GATLING GUN											
SECONDARY ATTACK MELEE SMASH											

PROTEAN HYBRID

A large humanoid combat chassis built by AIM under the direction of Kearson DeWitt. It is a synthesis of a human operator and PROTEAN technology. You first run into one of these enemies in Mission 4.

SPECIAL ABILITY
Capable of regenerating health using PROTEAN technology

HEALTH											
DAMAGE — MAIN ATTACK CHEST BEAM											
SECONDARY ATTACK PROTEAN BOMB											

ARC ARMIGER

A gigantic six-legged combat machine built by AIM, with an integral arc reactor (hence the name) and PROTEAN technology throughout. It is only found as the final boss in mission 6.

SPECIAL ABILITY
When damaged enough it releases turrets that have several types of attacks to defend itself while it uses PROTEAN technology to repair itself; Additionally, if a target is on the ground the Armiger is capable of stomping it

HEALTH											
DAMAGE — MAIN ATTACK MAIN GUN											
SECONDARY ATTACK MISSILE BARRAGE											

BATTERY

They fire volleys of homing missiles and have hover capability. These enemies are tough to take down. Use their missiles against them and bombard them with heavy weaponry.

SPECIAL ABILITY
None

HEALTH

MAIN ATTACK
MISSILE BARRAGE

SECONDARY ATTACK
NONE

DAMAGE

DYNAMO AND SILO

An AIM drone based on its work developing the Crimson Dynamo. This large humanoid drone has the attraction and repulsion powers of the Crimson Dynamo, as well as some of his melee and ranged electrical attacks. The Silo variant carries a single heavy cruise missile on its back. These are encountered during Mission 7. Take down their cruise missiles before they hit their target.

SPECIAL ABILITY
None

HEALTH

MAIN ATTACK
SILO MISSILE

SECONDARY ATTACK
MELEE ATTACK

DAMAGE

DEWITT'S HYBRID

The personal PROTEAN Hybrid unit of Kearson DeWitt, it is wired into the 600-foot battle chassis of ULTIMO, serving as its central control unit.

SPECIAL ABILITY
None

HEALTH

MAIN ATTACK
MELEE ATTACK

SECONDARY ATTACK
TURRETS

DAMAGE

ENEMIES

RESEARCH

Completing missions awards you Field Data. Field Data is spent at the Research screens to improve the Iron Man and War Machine suits with upgrades and new inventions. You can upgrade Ammunition, Weapons, and Combat Programs. You can also purchase modules that enhance weapons. After researching upgrades, select the Fabrication menu to load the desired ammunition and attach modules to your weapons.

THE COST OF UPGRADES

To invent everything, you must earn 62,671,000 Field Data.

FABRICATION

After researching Ammunition and Modules (see following pages), you must then go to Fabrication to add them to the weapons. For each weapon, you can fabricate four different versions. This way you can easily switch between your favorite setups.

The following tables show which weapons can be upgraded with each type of Ammunition and Module.

Ammunition

WEAPON	STANDARD	CONCUSSIVE	EXPLOSIVE	PIERCING	THERMITE	PULSE	LIGHTNING
Minigun	•	•	•	•		•	
Repulsor	•	•	•	•			
UniBeam							
Blaster	•	•	•	•			
Shotgun	•	•	•	•			
Rocket	•	•	•		•	•	•
Missiles	•	•	•	•	•	•	•
Laser	•	•	•	•			

Modules

WEAPON	EFFICIENCY	DAMAGE	HYBRID	FIRE RATE	PROTEAN	ULTIMATE
Minigun	•	•	•	•	•	•
Repulsor	•	•	•			•
UniBeam						
Shotgun/Blaster	•	•	•	•	•	•
Rocket		•	•	•	•	•
Missiles		•	•	•	•	•
Laser	•	•	•	•	•	•

STANDARD

Standard is the default ammunition found in every weapon. It has no modifiers.

WEAPONS THAT USE STANDARD AMMUNITION

Minigun	Shotgun	Missiles
Repulsor	Blaster	Laser
	Rocket	

field data needed: 1,860,000

AMMUNITION

CONCUSSIVE

Concussive ammunition can stagger or stun enemies in a small area around its impact point, but deals less damage than Standard ammunition.

WEAPONS THAT USE CONCUSSIVE AMMUNITION

Minigun	Shotgun	Missiles
Repulsor	Blaster	Laser
	Rocket	

field data needed: 10,000

EXPLOSIVE

Explosive ammunition deals splash damage to anything near its point of impact.

WEAPONS THAT USE EXPLOSIVE AMMUNITION

Minigun	Blaster	Laser
Repulsor	Rocket	
Shotgun	Missiles	

field data needed: 651,000

PULSE

Pulse ammunition accelerates towards its target, doing more damage the further it travels.

WEAPONS THAT USE PULSE AMMUNITION

Minigun	Rocket	Missiles

field data needed: 28,000

THERMITE

Thermite ammunition deals less initial damage, but continues to deal damage over time resulting in more damage overall. Only works with missiles and rockets.

WEAPONS THAT USE THERMITE AMMUNITION

Rocket	Missiles	

field data needed: 1,860,000

PIERCING

Piercing ammunition deals slightly less damage than Standard ammunition but will go through multiple enemies while dealing damage to each.

WEAPONS THAT USE PIERCING AMMUNITION

Minigun	Shotgun	Missiles
Repulsor	Blaster	Laser
	Rocket	

field data needed: 80,000

LIGHTNING

Lightning ammunition releases an electrical charge from its point of impact that can arc to nearby targets.

WEAPONS THAT USE LIGHTNING AMMUNITION

Rocket	Missiles	

field data required: 5,314,000

RESEARCH

MODULAR ENHANCEMENTS

EFFICIENCY MODULE

The Efficiency module either increases the clip size of a weapon, or extends the amount of time the weapon can be fired before recharging.

field data needed: 10,000

HYBRID MODULE

A Hybrid module increases a weapon's damage output and rate of fire. It is less effective in each area than the specialized modules, but the overall combination is impressive.

available for purchase after: mission 6
field data needed: 1,860,000

FIRING RATE MODULE

The Firing Rate module accelerates cooling and cycling mechanisms in weapons, improving their rates of fire.

field data needed: 80,000

PROTEAN MODULE

A modified PROTEAN colony in this module fabricates ammunition at a rapid pace.

field data needed: 15,182,000

DAMAGE MODULE

The Damage module accelerates projectiles and focuses energy bursts, greatly increasing the damage on impact.

field data needed: 228,000

ULTIMATE MODULE

The Ultimate module focuses the suit's entire power system and ammunition store into each shot fired, massively increasing the damage dealt.

field data needed: 15,182,000

CLOSE COMBAT PROGRAMS - IRON MAN

These programs are loaded into Iron Man's armor to give him certain fighting styles for each mission. The close combat programs can be upgraded through two improved stages: Advanced and Ultimate. Upgrading Close Combat programs adds additional moves.

Hurricane

Field Data Needed for Advanced: 10,000

Field Data Needed for Ultimate: 228,000

Iron Man uses this close combat program to devastate a single target with quick and repeated strikes with elbows and knees.

Dragon

Field Data Needed for Advanced: 28,000

Field Data Needed for Ultimate: 651,000

Iron Man uses kicks and lunges in this high-impact fighting style to stun foes.

Shield Power

Field Data Needed for Advanced: 80,000

Field Data Needed for Ultimate: 1,860,000

Iron Man uses his shield emitters to tackle multiple enemies in close combat.

CLOSE COMBAT PROGRAMS - WAR MACHINE

These programs are loaded into War Machine's armor to give him certain fighting styles for each mission. The close combat programs can be upgraded through two improved stages: Advanced and Ultimate. Upgrading Close Combat programs adds additional moves.

War Machine

Field Data Needed for Advanced: 10,000

Field Data Needed for Ultimate: 228,000

War Machine uses his weapons (including Laser Blade) to focus damage on a single target.

Brawler

Field Data Needed for Advanced: 28,000

Field Data Needed for Ultimate: 651,000

War Machine uses a mix of street fighting moves to stun enemies.

Brute Force

Field Data Needed for Advanced: 80,000

Field Data Needed for Ultimate: 1,860,000

War Machine's Brute Force program damages all nearby enemies. It's a bit slow but can devastate enemies so long as they don't interrupt it.

ROCKET LAUNCHER

clip size: 1 - reload time: 9 secs

This weapon's heavy rockets are effective against stationary targets. Each rocket is unguided but deals tremendous damage. Upgrades affect both War Machine and Iron Man.

RANK	REQUIRED FIELD DATA	DAMAGE (10 POINT SCALE)
MK I	0	5
MK II	80,000	7
MK III	1,860,000	9

AMMUNITION TYPES	AVAILABLE MODULES
Standard, Concussive, Explosive, Pierce, Thermite, Pulse, Lightning	Damage, Hybrid, Fire Rate, Protean, Ultimate

LASER

clip size: 25 - reload time: 3.1 seconds

This high-intensity laser cuts through almost anything with sustained application. It fires as long as the trigger is held, or until its capacitor runs dry. The capacitor recharges at any time the weapon is not in use.

RANK	REQUIRED FIELD DATA	DAMAGE (10 POINT SCALE)
MK I	0	3
MK II	28,000	5
MK III	1,860,000	7

AMMUNITION TYPES	AVAILABLE MODULES
Standard, Concussive, Explosive, Pierce	Efficiency, Damage, Hybrid, Fire Rate, Protean, Ultimate

BLASTERS

clip size: 5 - reload time: 6.5 seconds

An energy attack that is devastating at close range but its dam Upgrading Blasters also upgrades War Machine's Shotguns.

RANK	REQUIRED FIELD DATA	DAMAGE (10 POINT SCALE)
MK I	0	6
MK II	10,000	8
MK III	228,000	10

AMMUNITION TYPES	AVAILABLE MODULES
Standard, Concussive, Explosive, Pierce	Efficiency, Damage, Hybrid, Fire Rate, Protean, Ultimate

MISSILE LAUNCHER

clip size: 6 - reload time: 9 seconds

This weapon fires volleys of guided missiles. Hold the Fire button to lock on to multiple targets and release to fire. Upgrades affect both War Machine and Iron Man.

RANK	REQUIRED FIELD DATA	DAMAGE (10 POINT SCALE)
MK I	0	5
MK II	651,000	7
MK III	5,314,000	8

AMMUNITION TYPES	AVAILABLE MODULES
Standard, Concussive, Explosive, Pierce, Thermite, Pulse, Lightning	Damage, Hybrid, Fire Rate, Protean, Ultimate

UNIBEAM

This blast of arc reactor power fires from the center of Iron Man's chest. Hold both Fire buttons to charge it up to deal additional damage. You can charge it up to 3 seconds.

RANK	REQUIRED FIELD DATA	DAMAGE (10 POINT SCALE)
MK I	0	8
MK II	228,000	10
MK III	5,314,000	12

AVAILABLE MODULES
None

NO AMMO UPGRADES

The Unibeam is already an incredibly powerful weapon and thus does not use any ammunition types to modify its damage output.

REPULSOR

clip size: unlimited - reload time: 0

Iron Man's palm-mounted Repulsors can be used as weapons as well as propulsion. Holding the fire button charges the blast before firing. Charged shots can stagger enemies. It never runs out of ammunition and never overheats. You can recharge it up to 1 second.

RANK	REQUIRED FIELD DATA	DAMAGE (10 POINT SCALE)
MK I	0	3
MK II	10,000	6
MK III	228,000	8

AMMUNITION TYPES	AVAILABLE MODULES
Standard, Concussive, Explosive, Pierce	Damage, Hybrid, Ultimate

ROCKET LAUNCHER

This weapon's heavy rockets are effective against stationary targets. Each rocket is unguided but deals tremendous damage. Upgrades affect both War Machine and Iron Man.

RANK	REQUIRED FIELD DATA	DAMAGE (10 POINT SCALE)
MK I	0	5
MK II	80,000	7
MK III	1,860,000	9

AMMUNITION TYPES	AVAILABLE MODULES
Standard, Concussive, Explosive, Pierce, Thermite, Pulse, Lightning	Damage, Hybrid, Fire Rate, Protean, Ultimate

MINIGUN

clip size: 25 - reload time: 3.1 seconds

War Machine's Minigun fires 20mm rounds at a high rate of speed for as long as fire button is held until it overheats. The Minigun's heat level decreases while it is not being fired.

RANK	REQUIRED FIELD DATA	DAMAGE (10 POINT SCALE)
MK I	0	3
MK II	10,000	5
MK III	651,000	7

AMMUNITION TYPES	AVAILABLE MODULES
Standard, Concussive, Explosive, Pierce, Pulse	Efficiency, Damage, Hybrid, Fire Rate, Protean, Ultimate

MISSILE LAUNCHER

clip size: 6 - reload time: 9 seconds

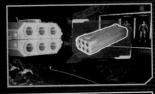

This weapon fires volleys of guided missiles. Hold the Fire button to lock on to multiple targets and release to fire. Upgrades affect both War Machine and Iron Man.

RANK	REQUIRED FIELD DATA	DAMAGE (10 POINT SCALE)
MK I	0	5
MK II	651,000	7
MK III	5,314,000	9

AMMUNITION TYPES	AVAILABLE MODULES
Standard, Concussive, Explosive, Pierce, Thermite, Pulse, Lightning	Damage, Hybrid, Fire Rate, Protean, Ultimate

SHOTGUNS

clip size: 5 - reload time: 6.5 seconds

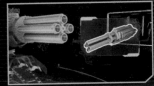

Shotguns are devastating at close range but the damage they deal is spread over an area instead of concentrated. Upgrading Shotguns also upgrades Iron Man's Blasters.

RANK	REQUIRED FIELD DATA	DAMAGE (10 POINT SCALE)
MK I	0	6
MK II	10,000	8
MK III	228,000	10

AMMUNITION TYPES	AVAILABLE MODULES
Standard, Concussive, Explosive, Pierce	Efficiency, Damage, Hybrid, Fire Rate, Protean, Ultimate

1 THE STARK ARCHIVES

MISSION DESCRIPTION

Iron Man is knocked out inside Stark Archives after responding to a warning from James Rhodes. Roxxon has initiated an attack on the archives in an attempt to get to the Dataspine and steal Stark tech and a copy of JARVIS. Iron Man comes to, but with limited abilities. He must reach the Dataspine and activate the shield generator.

PRIMARY OBJECTIVE

Stop the Roxxon raid on the Stark Archives. Prevent the theft of dangerous technology and data.

MAX FIELD DATA

MISSION	21600
OPPOSITION	1320
SUIT INTEGRITY	1080
TOTAL	24000

RECOMMENDED LOADOUT

IRON MAN

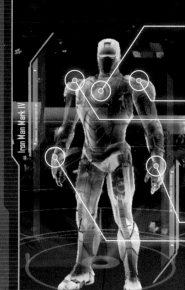

Iron Man Mark IV

Chest
• Unibeam: MKI

Left Shoulder
• Missile Launcher: MKI
• Ammunition: Standard
• Module: None

Right Shoulder
• Rocket Launcher: MKI
• Ammunition: Standard
• Module: None

Left Wrist
• Blasters: MKI
• Ammunition: Standard
• Module: None

Right Wrist
• Repulsors: MKI
• Ammunition: Standard
• Module: None

WAR MACHINE

War Machine

Left Shoulder
• Minigun: MKI
• Ammunition: Standard
• Module: None

Right Shoulder
• Missile Launcher: MKI
• Ammunition: Standard
• Module: None

Left Wrist
• Shotgun: MKI
• Ammunition: Standard
• Module: None

Right Wrist
• Rocket Launcher: MKI
• Ammunition: Standard
• Module: None

ACTIVATE THE AUXILIARY SHIELD GENERATOR

Once you have control of Iron Man, your first objective is to activate the shield generator. Run ahead and hover up through the hole in the ceiling. Head across the next floor and into another hole.

▶ Hover over the wreckage to find an exit.

▶ Get your bearings and head towards the hole in the ceiling ahead.

Hack the Security Panel to Open the Door

On the next floor, fly over to the panel near the door. The EMP has scrambled the passcodes so you must hack into Stark's computer to get it open. At the security panel press the indicated button to fill the meter. Once the door is open proceed into the next room.

▶ Tony must hack into his own computer to open the door.

Stop Illicit Data Transfers by Roxxon "Wing" Drones

In the next room, four Drones are transferring information from Stark Industries computers and just in time, Jarvis gets Iron Man's Repulsors back online. Target the closest Drone and take it down with Repulsors. The next enemy is automatically targeted, so continue to fire until all are eliminated.

Defeat Roxxon Forces

Head toward the exit, where more Roxxon Wings appear. Take them down before entering the next room. A few more wings are found here with a Patrol Drone. Take down the Roxxon Wings with some quick Repulsor blasts before engaging the Patrol Drones in melee combat.

▶ Use Iron Man's Repulsors to stop the Drones from stealing the data.

▶ Take down the drones with some quick Repulsors.

▶ Iron Man's fists are effective against the Patrol Drones.

WATCH FOR THE GLOW

Let Iron Man block the soldier's attack, then when you see the blue glow, press the Counter Attack button to stun it. Now you can freely take down the enemy with a few more punches.

Two more Patrol Drones come through another door. Take them down with some melee attacks or Repulsors. If you see an icon of a controller button appear on one of the soldiers, you can get close and press that button to reprogram it to fight for you.

▶ Two more Patrol Drones join the fight.

Hack the Security Panel to Open the Door

Another security panel must be hacked before reaching the shield generator. Press the appropriate button to open the door.

▶ *Hack another security panel.*

Defeat Roxxon Forces

In the next room Iron Man reaches the shield generator, only to find more Grappler Drones destroying it. That means it's time for plan B. Use the Unibeam on the drone to take it down with one shot.

Two more Grappler Drones await Iron Man on the other side of the generator. Take them out with some ranged Repulsor shots or get in close with some melee shots.

▶ *The Unibeam makes quick work of the enemy.*

▶ *Defeat the rest of the Roxxon forces.*

MISSION 1

TURNING FOES INTO FRIENDS

If you get to the first drone quickly enough, you can grapple and hack it to turn them against each other. Watch the fight or help out your new friend with some Repulsor shots.

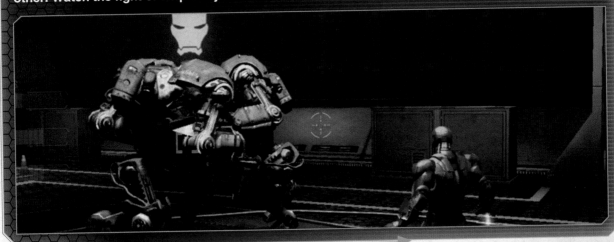

Get to the Dataspine Core

Once the drones are eliminated, hover to the second floor and look for the yellow objective marker at the exit. Enter the doorway to complete Iron Man's part of Mission 1.

New Achievement

Reaching this part of the game gets you the first achievement, Shake It Off.

▶ Get to the Dataspine Core.

INTERCEPT THE ROXXON DROPSHIPS

As Iron Man attempts to blow up the Dataspine, War Machine must keep the Roxxon forces away. Roxxon Dropships bring more Patrol Drones into the battle. Your first objective as War Machine is to intercept these ships and destroy them before they drop more forces.

Tony's Dataspine Overload Progress shows up as a horizontal progress bar on the top of the HUD. War Machine must hold off the Roxxon forces until this bar is filled. The first Dropship shows up on the radar. Target it and initiate flight to get to it as quickly as possible. Once War machine is within range, hit it with some missiles and shots from the Minigun.

▶ **Tony's Dataspine Overload Progress shows up on your HUD.**

▶ *Get to the Dropships as soon as possible to keep them from unloading troops.*

Two more appear on the horizon. Immediately target one and head that way. Hold the Missile fire button and target each to launch missiles at both. Finish them off with the Minigun

New Achievement

Preventing the first wave of Roxxon Dropships from deploying their drones earns another achievement, Not In My House.

▶ *Use War Machine's Missiles and Minigun to finish off the Dropships.*

PROTECT THE DATASPINE FROM THE ROXXON "WING" DRONES

At this point Roxxon Wing Drones start flying in from all directions in an attempt to retrieve more data. Another bar appears below the top bar called Stark Archive Download. This shows the progress of the Roxxon "Wing" Drones. This must not fill up before Tony's Dataspine Overload Progress bar.

▶ *Another progress bar appears titled Stark Archive Download.*

Watch the radar and spot the red dots with the yellow outline. These are the Wing Drones that War Machine must keep from downloading more data. Fly towards the first ones and take them down with some Minigun fire.

▶ Dispose of the Wings quickly.

SAVE YOUR MISSILES

Do not waste your Missiles on the Roxxon Wing Drones. A few bullets from the Minigun dispatches each of them. The Grappler Drones that join the fight are better targets for the Missiles.

Once you take out a group of Wing Drones, immediately look for the next ones. Fly to get there faster and hit them with Minigun fire.

▶ Take down the Wings quickly to prevent them from stealing too much information.

Also keep an eye out for Dropships. If you can get to them quickly enough, you can keep them from dropping more troops. If they successfully make a drop, use War Machine's combat skills on the soldiers and hit the Grappler Drones with missiles.

▶ Take down the Dropships quickly for an easier fight.

Continue to circle around the tower targeting each group of Wing Drones and eliminating them with the Minigun. Use the Radar and the Target button to find them more easily. Once Tony finishes with the detonation sequence, a cutscene begins and Mission 1 is complete.

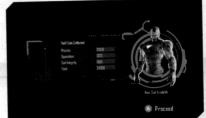

After each mission, you are awarded Field Data depending on how well you did throughout the mission. Once a mission is complete, you can play it again as much as you want to earn more Field Data.

NEW SUIT AVAILABLE

Completing Mission 1 unlocks the Mark VI Iron Man Armor, an advanced variant of the Mark IV. At Headquarters, try your hand at some Research. With only 24,000 Field Data, there isn't much that you can afford. Try out the Efficiency Module or upgrade a few Weapons or Combat Programs. Add any new Ammunition and Modules to your Weapons by selecting Fabrication at Headquarters.

New Achievements

Completing the mission earns two new achievements, Access Denied and Mark VI.

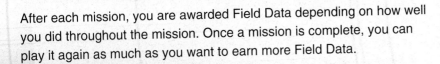

2 RUSSIA AND ROXXON

MISSION DESCRIPTION

Following the leads from the first mission, it's determined that General Valentin Shatalov, a separatist rebelling against the Russian government he believes has gone soft, is the likely power behind the Roxxon operation at the Stark Archives. Our heroes join S.H.I.E.L.D. in helping defeat Shatalov's insurrection, including a battle cruiser full of Armigers.

RECOMMENDED LOADOUT

IRON MAN

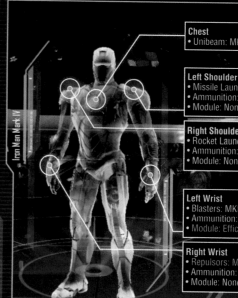

Iron Man Mark IV

Chest
• Unibeam: MKI

Left Shoulder
• Missile Launcher: MKI
• Ammunition: Standard
• Module: None

Right Shoulder
• Rocket Launcher: MKI
• Ammunition: Standard
• Module: None

Left Wrist
• Blasters: MKI
• Ammunition: Standard
• Module: Efficiency

Right Wrist
• Repulsors: MKII
• Ammunition: Standard
• Module: None

WAR MACHINE

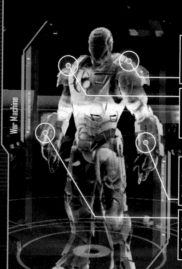

War Machine

Left Shoulder
• Missile Launcher: MKI
• Ammunition: Standard
• Module: None

Right Shoulder
• Minigun: MKI
• Ammunition: Standard
• Module: Efficiency

Left Wrist
• Shotgun: MKI
• Ammunition: Standard
• Module: Efficiency

Right Wrist
• Rocket Launcher: MKI
• Ammunition: Standard
• Module: None

PRIMARY OBJECTIVE

Defeat General Shatalov's insurrectionists and prevent the deployment of Roxxon "Armiger" battle platforms.

MAX FIELD DATA

MISSION	45,000
OPPOSITION	2,750
SUIT INTEGRITY	2,250
TOTAL	50,000

ESCORT THE S.H.I.E.L.D. STRIKE FORCE THROUGH THE CANYON

Iron Man or War Machine must escort S.H.I.E.L.D. transports through a Russian canyon while protecting them from helicopters, tanks, turrets, and other Roxxon forces. Fly to the head of the transports, but don't stray too far. If you do, you receive a warning to return to the mission area.

▶ Fly to the head of the convoy.

There are four helicopters flying around with tanks and turrets lined along each side. Once you reach the bridge target the nearby turret and hit it with the Repulsor and a rocket.

TONY OR RHODEY

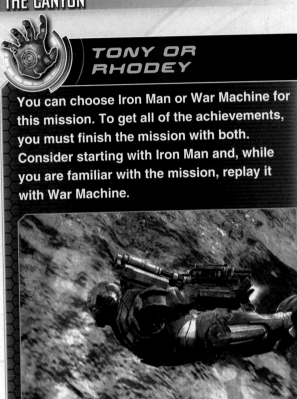

You can choose Iron Man or War Machine for this mission. To get all of the achievements, you must finish the mission with both. Consider starting with Iron Man and, while you are familiar with the mission, replay it with War Machine.

Reloading

Escort the S.H.I.E.L.D. strike force through the canyon

▶ Hit the nearby turrets and tanks before the helicopters take notice.

Get the pesky helicopters off the transports with some missiles and Repulsor shots. Use rockets against the stationary targets on the ground whenever available.

▶ *Keep the helicopters off of the Transports.*

▶ *Use rockets on the stationary ground targets.*

Once the helicopters have been destroyed, quickly take out the rest of the forces on the ground. When they're ready, launch a salvo of missiles at an enemy, then immediately switch to a new target.

▶ *Rid the area of Russian troops.*

As the convoy moves ahead, a Roxxon Battery appears. Hit it with weapons fire until it is vulnerable. When it's vulnerable, grapple and reprogram it. Quickly fly back to the front of the transports.

▶ *Grapple the vulnerable battery and reprogram it.*

ELIMINATE THE ROXXON "ARMIGER" BATTLE PLATFORM

A Roxxon Armiger blocks the transports' path and only Iron Man or War Machine can remove it. Target the enormous, four-legged fighting machine and its health bar appears at the top of the HUD.

Hit it with everything in your arsenal. As soon as the missiles and rocket are ready, let them go. When you're controlling Iron Man, use the Unibeam whenever it is available.

▶ Deflect the missiles back at the Armiger.

▶ Use the Unibeam when available.

The Roxxon Armiger has its own array of weapons. The first one you see is its missile salvo. The usual alarm sounds when targeted, so be ready to counter it when you hear the alarm. Press the indicated button as soon as it appears on screen to deflect the missiles.

The Armiger's laser is easier to see coming, but tougher to avoid. It shoots a beam at your hero. Dodge above or below the shot to avoid taking damage.

▶ *Avoid the laser by dodging up or down.*

It also has a Pulse weapon that fires a slew of electromagnetic spheres. These are slow moving and easily avoided.

Watch out for its machine gun fire. It doesn't cause much damage, but it does knock down your hero. Dodge from side to side to avoid its fire.

▶ *Dodge the Pulses.*

▶ *Its machine gun fire is just a nuisance.*

Stay on the move to avoid its fire and keep hitting it with your heavy weapons until it becomes vulnerable—indicated by the button that appears on its top. Hover down to the Armiger and press the indicated button to finish it off.

Roxxon Armiger

Reloading

Eliminate the Roxxon "Armiger" battle platform

▶ *Keep hitting it until it becomes vulnerable.*

Roxxon Armiger

Eliminate the Roxxon "Armiger" battle platform

▶ *Finish off the Armiger.*

RESUME S.H.I.E.L.D. STRIKE FORCE ESCORT

Continue down the canyon leading the way for the transports, until you see two batteries heading your way. Immediately target them with missiles and finish them off before they get to the transports. If one becomes vulnerable, take that opportunity to reprogram it.

Around the next turn, the convoy is attacked by a helicopters, turrets, and tanks. Take down the helicopters with missiles and Repulsors. When available, use rockets on the turrets and tanks.

▶ Take down the helicopters first.

▶ Focus on the stationary targets on the ground next.

ELIMINATE THE ANTI-AIR DEFENSES PROTECTING THE TUNNEL ENTRANCE

The S.H.I.E.L.D. strike force hangs back as Iron Man or War Machine continues ahead into the middle of some anti-air defenses. The easiest way out of this is to use their missiles against them. Once you hear the alarm, be ready with the appropriate button press to deflect their shots.

▶ Be ready to deflect their missiles back at them.

Helicopters, tanks, and patrol drones also join the fray to make your job tougher. Hit the helicopter with missiles while waiting for the patrol drones to attack. When your hero blocks their attack, counter with some melee attacks.

▶ Hit the helicopter with a barrage of missiles.

▶ Counter the patrol drones with melee attacks.

MAKING FRIENDS

If you see a Patrol Drone that is vulnerable, reprogram it so that it fights for your side.

Eliminate the anti-air defenses protecting the tunnel entrance.

▶ More Russian Soldiers await the team after the tunnel.

ENTER THE TUNNEL

After the turrets are gone, the transports start moving for the tunnel. Defeat the remaining enemy forces and lead the way into the tunnel.

LOCATE THE ENTRANCE TO THE COMMAND BUILDING

Use the Repulsor or Minigun on the soldiers and hit the tanks with heavy weaponry to clear out this initial area. Your hero's special ability becomes available, but you should save it for later when the fight gets tougher.

Your suit's special ability (Invincibility or Omega System) is ready for use!

▶ Wipeout the soldiers and tanks in this first area.

Enter the tunnel

▶ Enter the tunnel once the enemy has been eliminated.

On the other side of the tunnel, the S.H.I.E.L.D. forces are greeted by more Russian soldiers and Roxxon Drones. The Transports unload their troops and give air support to the cause. After reaching the docks, you must now take down the battle cruiser that holds more Armigers.

New Achievement

If you reach the tunnel while losing no more than one transport, you earn the Full Flight achievement.

NEW ACHIEVEMENT

This scenario makes for a great opportunity to get the Unnecessary Force Achievement when playing as Iron Man. Use Unibeam on one of the defenseless soldiers to earn it.

MISSION 2

Move out to the middle of the docks and protect the transports from the helicopters before working on the anti-air tanks that surround the area. The command building, the next objective, is marked on the radar, but it is best to clear out the enemy first.

Work around the perimeter of the docks, taking out the ground forces as you go. Keep an eye in the sky too, as Patrol Drones and more helicopters join the fight. Dodge the incoming fire and clear the docks with missiles and rockets. Eliminate the Patrol Drones with counter and melee attacks.

▶ Dodge the fire from the Russians.

▶ Use melee abilities on the Patrol Drones.

ACCESS THE COMMAND BUILDING TERMINAL

As you reach the command building, use the hero's heavy weapons on the tank nearby to clear the way. The next door is protected by a shield and the generators that power it appear on the radar.

▶ Take out the tank next to the command building.

▶ The generators that power the shield appear on the radar.

ENTER THE POWER BUILDING AND DISABLE THE GENERATORS

Fly straight across the docks toward the marked building. Bust through one of the doors and take care of the two Grappler Drones inside. Destroy the two generators—one on the bottom floor and another up the steps.

Enter the power building and disable the generators

Return to the Command Building and hack the computer inside to gain access to the battle cruiser's bridge. Exit the building and take out the Roxxon Patrol Drones around the docks.

▶ *Defeat the two Patrol Drones outside.*

ENTER THE BRIDGE AT THE TOP OF THE BATTLE CRUISER AND OPEN THE DEPLOYMENT DOORS

Fly up to the bridge of the battle cruiser and enter the door. Use the control panel on the wall to open the deployment door. A Roxxon Armiger emerges from the battle cruiser.

▶ *Fly to the bridge.*

▶ *Use the control panel to open the deployment doors.*

ELIMINATE THE ROXXON "ARMIGER" BATTLE PLATFORM

Head back outside and battle the Armiger just as before, although this time you get some help from the S.H.I.E.L.D. transports. Deflect the Armiger's missiles and avoid its lasers and pulses.

▶ Battle the Roxxon Armiger.

▶ Avoid the various weapon fire from the Armiger.

Continue to pelt it with everything you have until it becomes vulnerable. Hover down to its back and take it down with a final blow.

▶ Finish off the vulnerable Armiger.

New Achievement

As long as 10 S.H.I.E.L.D. units have survived the battle for the docks, you earn the Area Secured Achievement.

Iron Man 2   7:32 AM

Area Secured   20 Ⓖ 🔒

Achievement Description
At least 10 S.H.I.E.L.D. units survive the battle for the docks.

Ⓑ Back

LOCATE AND DESTROY THE TESLA SHIELD GENERATORS

Enter through the deployment doors of the battle cruiser and turn to the right. As the door opens two Grappler Drones appear. If one becomes vulnerable, reprogram it to help your cause or just take them down.

▶ *Two Grappler Drones emerge from the doorway.*

The next room holds the first Tesla Shield generators and a few Patrol Drones. Counter their attacks and defeat them with melee attacks and weapon fire. Destroy the generator before heading back into the main cargo hold.

▶ *Defeat the Patrol Drones.*

▶ *Destroy the first shield generator.*

Take down the two Patrol Drones that appear from the other side. Enter the opposite door and look out for Grappler Drones. If it's possible, reprogram a few to help you out. Otherwise try to keep your distance while launching a barrage of projectiles at them. Once they are eliminated, destroy the second generator to lower the shield. Exit the door just as S.H.I.E.L.D. destroys the battle cruiser.

▶ Four Grappler Drones protect the second shield generator.

▶ Destroy the generator to lower the shield.

New Achievements

Completing Mission 2 earns you the Deportation Achievement. Plus if you complete it with both Iron Man and War Machine, you get the Two Man Army Achievement.

NEW SUIT AVAILABLE

Completing Mission 2 with at least 48,500 Field Data unlocks the Iron Man Mark II suit. Playing through Mission 2 twice awards you 100,000 Field Data. Take this time to do some research and fabrication.

Suit Selection

Iron Man Mark II

Tony constructed the Iron Man Mark II to explore flight potential. It was later converted into the War Machine armor.

2 / 4

◀ ▶ Navigate Ⓐ Select Ⓑ Back

3 THE CRIMSON DYNAMO

MISSION DESCRIPTION

With the Armiger threat quelled, it's time to take on Shatalov and his Crimson Dyanamo armor. The heroes must infiltrate his Tesla facility and defeat the rogue general.

PRIMARY OBJECTIVE

Locate Natasha and defeat General Shatalov in his remote Tesla power facility.

MAX FIELD DATA

MISSION	144,000
OPPOSITION	8,800
SUIT INTEGRITY	7,200
TOTAL	160,000

RECOMMENDED LOADOUT

IRON MAN

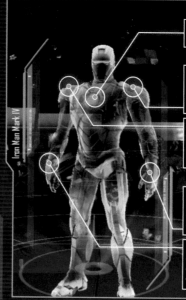

Iron Man Mark IV

Chest
• Unibeam: MKI

Left Shoulder
• Missile Launcher: MKI
• Ammunition: Pulse
• Module: None

Right Shoulder
• Rocket Launcher: MKI
• Ammunition: Pulse
• Module: None

Left Wrist
• Blasters: MKI
• Ammunition: Standard
• Module: Efficiency

Right Wrist
• Repulsors: MKII
• Ammunition: Standard
• Module: None

WAR MACHINE

War Machine

Left Shoulder
• Missile Launcher: MKI
• Ammunition: Pulse
• Module: None

Right Shoulder
• Minigun: MKI
• Ammunition: Standard
• Module: Efficiency

Left Wrist
• Shotgun: MKI
• Ammunition: Standard
• Module: Efficiency

Right Wrist
• Rocket Launcher: MKI
• Ammunition: Pulse
• Module: None

LOCATE THE TESLA REACTOR

Your hero infiltrates the Tesla factory through a vent only to be confronted by a pack of four Grappler Drones. Hover into the air to avoid their hard hits, but watch out for the long arm that can pull in your character and deal some damage.

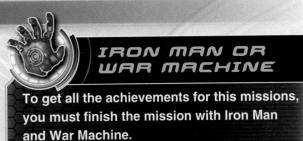

IRON MAN OR WAR MACHINE

To get all the achievements for this missions, you must finish the mission with Iron Man and War Machine.

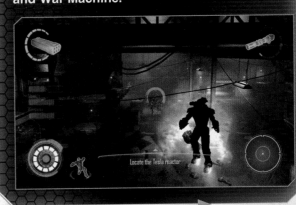

▶ *Take flight to avoid the Grappler Drones.*

Take any opportunity you get to reprogram vulnerable drones. This can make the fight a tad easier. Take down the four Grappler Drones and more appear on the other side of the factory floor.

▶ *Reprogram any vulnerable Grappler Drones.*

MISSION 3

Immediately target the new drones and hit them with missiles—eliminating them before they reach your hero. Once they're defeated, fly to the exit located in far right corner.

Use the control panel on the wall to open the door. Grappler and Patrol Drones appear; quickly dodge behind them, so they are all in view. Counter any attacks by the Patrol Drones and hit the Grappler Drones with heavy weaponry.

▶ *Head to the exit in the far corner.*

▶ *Counter any attacks by the Patrol Drones.*

BLOW THE REACTOR ROOM DOORS OPEN

Move down the hallway until a few additional Grappler Drones appear. Take them down with some long distance missiles before busting through the door to the reactor room.

▶ *Eliminate the two Grappler Drones.*

DESTROY THE TESLA REACTOR'S STABILIZERS

The four stabilizers are located in the four corners of the reactor room, but do not fire on them yet. The Patrol and Grappler Drones in the room should be your first target.

▶ *Take out the Roxxon forces before targeting the stabilizers.*

After the enemies have been defeated, destroy the nearest stabilizers. Head to the other side of the room and take out the final stabilizers.

New Achievement

Destroy all four Tesla reactor stabilizers in less than 60 seconds to earn the Pulling the Plug Achievement.

ESCAPE BEFORE THE REACTOR EXPLODES

Without the stabilizers, the reactor will explode. A timer with 1:30 starts to count down, so immediately exit out the door and get ready to initiate flight.

Move around the corner and go into flight. Try to keep it straight as possible—making small adjustments so that your hero doesn't smack into the sides of the shaft. Continue in flight until a cinematic takes over and your hero emerges from the factory.

▶ *Escape the reactor explosion.*

▶ *Iron Man emerges from the Tesla factory just in time.*

▶ Hit the tanks with rockets and missiles.

Expect additional encounters with Russian and Roxxon forces on the way to the buildings ahead. Eliminate them quickly as there are helicopters to deal with as well.

ACCESS THE FACILITY SUBNET

Once outside, possible locations for the facility subnet appear on the radar. Your hero is greeted by Patrol Drones and tanks. Counter the Patrol Drones' attacks and hit the tanks with rockets and missiles before following the road.

▶ You must find the facility subnet.

▶ *Watch out for the helicopters.*

Hover above the buildings and take out the tanks, turret, Grappler Drones, and Patrol Drones. Enter the second building on the right and search for a computer. Bust inside and hack into the facility subnet to find the S.H.I.E.L.D. agent's location.

▶ *Gain access to this building to find the computer.*

▶ *Hack into the facility subnet.*

RESCUE NATASHA

Now the radar shows only one location—that of agent Natasha. There are many Russian and Roxxon forces between your location and hers. Helicopters, tanks, Grappler Drones, Patrol Drones, and even a few batteries get in the way.

▶ Exit the building and start eliminating the troops outside.

▶ Save your ammo when fighting the Patrol Drones.

MISSILE ALARM

Remember to be ready for incoming missiles. When the alarm sounds, press the indicated button to deflect them back at the targeted enemy.

DEFEAT THE ROXXON ARMIGER

While approaching the next group of buildings, your hero is knocked out of the air. There is a Roxxon Armiger guarding the building that holds Natasha.

▶ A Roxxon Armiger stands in the hero's way.

By this point you have fought at least two of these Armigers. Use the prior experience to defeat the enemy. Deflect the missiles back and avoid the lasers and pulses from the Armiger. Once vulnerable, finish it off with a final blow.

▶ *Deflect the missiles back at the Armiger.*

▶ *Avoid the lasers from the Armiger.*

DEFEND THE LANDING ZONE

▶ *Natasha and Iron Man need to defend the landing zone.*

▶ *Natasha mans an anti-air gun.*

Once the Armiger has been eliminated, your hero enters the building to get Natasha. A transporter is ready to extract her from the area, except there is one problem. Hordes of Russian and Roxxon forces are on their way. Natasha mans the big anti-air gun to help you defend the area. Natasha's health bar appears on the top of your HUD. If Natasha dies, the game is over.

Keep an eye on the radar and intercept each enemy as soon as you see the red dot. Natasha can hold her own, but she can get overwhelmed. If you see a red dot next to her spot on the radar quickly release your current target and target the enemy that harasses her.

Continue to move from target to target—taking them out until the transporter shows up and takes away Natasha.

▶ *Don't let Natasha become overwhelmed by the enemy.*

▶ *Take out the attacking forces until the transporter shows up.*

New Achievement

Destroy 37% of all destructible items in the outside portion of Mission 3 to earn the Anger Management Achievement. Destroy all of the rooftops and brick buildings with your rockets. Keep in mind that you can do this at both bases.

DESTROY THE POWER PROJECTORS ON THE TESLA TOWER

After rescuing Natasha, Iron Man and War Machine run into General Shatalov in his Crimson Dynamo suit. He hovers around the Tesla Tower drawing power from it. An electromagnetic shield keeps the heroes nearby.

▶ *Crimson Dynamo*

First your hero must destroy the three power projectors along the tower. Target each projector and take it out with shots from the Repulsor or Minigun. Try to keep the Crimson Dynamo in view as he attacks as you do so.

▶ Destroy the power projectors.

DEFEAT THE CRIMSON DYNAMO

Once the projectors are destroyed, focus your attention on the Crimson Dynamo. Try to stay on the opposite side of the tower and launch missiles at him every chance you get.

The Crimson Dynamo is occasionally powered up by the tower. Use this opportunity to move behind the tower.

▶ Stay on the opposite side of the tower when possible.

▶ Move behind the tower when the Crimson Dynamo starts to power up.

MISSION 3

The Crimson Dynamo is able to draw your hero close, then grab and slam him to the ground. If you notice your hero being drawn in, dodge in the opposite way to keep the boss from grabbing him. Again, try to keep the tower between your hero and the Crimson Dynamo.

INVINCIBLE IRON MAN

This is a good opportunity to use Iron Man's Invincibility. This saves quite a bit of health and allows Iron Man to engage in some close combat.

▶ Watch out for the grab.

▶ Dodge away from the Crimson Dynamo when close.

After your hero has taken the Crimson Dynamo's health down low enough, the other hero attempts to help by jumping on the boss's back. Your partner's health bar appears below the Crimson Dynamo health bar. This bar goes down quickly so you must be fast.

▶ Your partner attempts to help by jumping on the boss's back.

Launch everything you have at the boss, including the Unibeam, as quickly as possible. If you aren't fast enough, the Crimson Dynamo kills the one on his back, which ends the game. Once you successfully take down Crimson Dynamo, the mission ends.

▶ *Quickly launch everything at the boss.*

▶ *Finish off the Crimson Dynamo to save your partner.*

New Achievements

Completing the mission earns you the Power Outage Achievement. Plus if you complete it with both Iron Man and War Machine, you get the It Takes Two to Tangle Achievement.

NEW SUIT AVAILABLE

Completing Mission 3 with at least 155,200 Field Data unlocks the Classic Iron Man Mark I suit.

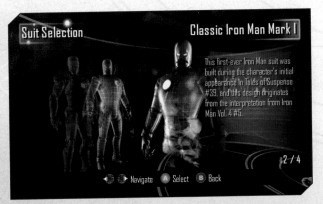

4 PROTEAN

MISSION DESCRIPTION

Tony realizes that DeWitt has stolen and implemented Stark's PROTEAN technology. The heroes raid the AIM facility where DeWitt was last known to be. The PROTEAN technology has gone haywire, and AIM troopers are fighting their own drones when they arrive.

PRIMARY OBJECTIVE

Shut down AIM's plans to use the stolen JARVIS source code and PROTEAN technology to create a rogue AI.

MAX FIELD DATA

MISSION	405,000
OPPOSITION	24,750
SUIT INTEGRITY	20,250
TOTAL	450,000

RECOMMENDED LOADOUT

IRON MAN

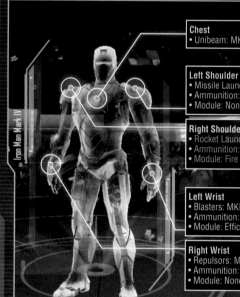

Iron Man Mark IV

Chest
• Unibeam: MKI

Left Shoulder
• Missile Launcher: MKI
• Ammunition: Standard
• Module: None

Right Shoulder
• Rocket Launcher: MKII
• Ammunition: Piercing
• Module: Fire Rate

Left Wrist
• Blasters: MKI
• Ammunition: Standard
• Module: Efficiency

Right Wrist
• Repulsors: MKII
• Ammunition: Standard
• Module: None

WAR MACHINE

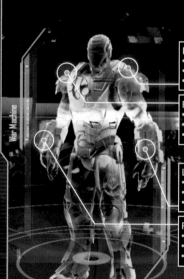

War Machine

Left Shoulder
• Missile Launcher: MKI
• Ammunition: Pulse
• Module: None

Right Shoulder
• Minigun: MKI
• Ammunition: Standard
• Module: Efficiency

Left Wrist
• Shotgun: MKI
• Ammunition: Standard
• Module: Efficiency

Right Wrist
• Rocket Launcher: MKII
• Ammunition: Piercing
• Module: Fire Rate

LOCATE DEWITT'S ARC REATORS

Your hero infiltrates the AIM facility in search of DeWitt's arc reactors. The first step is to hover over to the computer ahead and use it to locate the reactors. The door opens into an elevator

▶ Hover over to the computer ahead.

PLAY THROUGH WITH BOTH

To get all of the achievements, you must finish the mission with both Iron Man and War Machine.

ACTIVATE THE LOADING PLATFORM

Another computer sits in the middle of the elevator. Use it to activate the platform. Unfortunately, this sets off an alarm and activates a slew of laser triplines below.

Activate the loading platform

▶ Use the computer to activate the loading platform.

▶ Laser triplines make your hero's descent tricky.

PROCEED TO THE REACTOR ROOM

Start your descent down the elevator shaft being mindful of the triplines. Touching a laser doesn't cause too much damage but will make Wasps appear.

Proceed to the reactor room

New Achievement

Reach the bottom of the elevator shaft without touching a laser tripline to earn the Entrapment Achievement.

Once the hero reaches the bottom, several AIM Wasps and Patrol Drones attack. The Wasps go down easily with shots

▶ Hit the Wasps with the Minigun or Repulsor.

from your Minigun or Repulsor. Counter the Drones with melee attacks or nail them with some missiles.

▶ Counter the Patrol Drones.

Head down the corridor just until you can target the right set of turrets. There are four turrets on each side of the next door and you should avoid having both sets fire on you. Take out the four right turrets before entering the next room.
Immediately destroy the left turrets.

▶ *Stop where you can target the right turrets.*

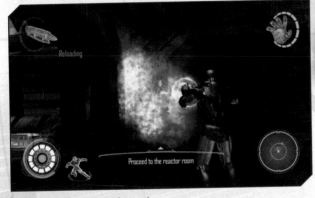

▶ *Destroy these turrets next.*

Bust through the door and head over to another computer. Hack it in an attempt to access the reactor room. Your hero is infected by a virus that takes out his flight systems.

PROCEED TO THE OBSERVATION AREA

The door opens to reveal the reactors. Several AIM Wasps, Grappler Drones, and Patrol Drones are fighting inside. Take out the first group of enemies before following the path of red dots to the exit.

▶ *A virus takes out the hero's flight systems.*

▶ *Take out the AIM forces in the reactor room.*

Once the enemy has been taken care of, bust through the door and continue to the observation area. Down the next hall, two Patrol Drones attack. Counter their attacks and eliminate them.

▶ Take out the AIM forces, before busting through the exit.

▶ Take down the Patrol Drones.

Crash through the next door but watch out for two more Patrol Drones. Beat them down before entering the observation area. At this point the virus takes out your hero's weapons systems.

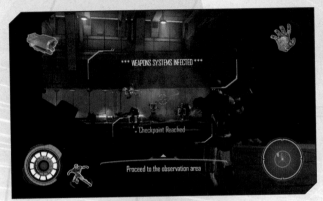

▶ Now your hero's weapons systems are infected.

DESTROY THE GENERATORS

Several AIM Wasps and Patrol Drones are there to greet your hero. Without weapons you must rely on melee abilities to take them down. Counter the Patrol Drones' attacks while dodging the shots from the Wasps. Get close to a Wasp and use the Grapple button to grab it and fling it at another enemy.

Once the room is clear of threats, approach the two generators and destroy them with melee attacks.

▶ Counter the Patrol Drones.

▶ Grab the Wasps and use them as projectile weapons.

▶ Destroy the generators.

CALL IN THE HELICARRIER STRIKE

This allows your hero to use the nearby computer to call in a strike from the Helicarrier. The strike has some unintended consequences!

► *Use the computer to call in the Helicarrier strike.*

LOCATE KEARSON DEWITT

Your hero comes to and it appears the blast rid his suit of the infection, while weapons and flight are restored. The new objective is to find Kearson DeWitt.

► *Weapons and flight are restored.*

Take out the pesky Wasps with the Minigun or Repulsor before heading down the hall. A Grappler Drone attacks along the way. Keep your distance and pump it full of missiles.

Return to the generator room where a hole has opened up on the other side. Drop down into the hole and through a door at the bottom.

Down the corridor, JARVIS warns of something in the distance. A PROTEAN Hybrid appears and runs toward your hero while firing some pulse shots. Deflect these back at it and dodge its big shots.

▷ *Deflect the pulses back at the PROTEAN Hybrid.*

▷ *Dodge electromagnetic weapon fire.*

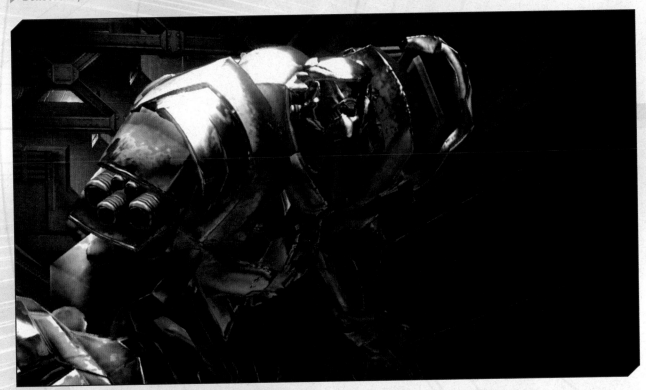

RUN

Launch everything you have at it until it slumps over and regenerates its health. At this point you have only one option—run! Once the next door opens, fly into the next room where your hero finds himself near a shock point assembly.

▷ *Take its health down until it slumps over.*

▷ *Flee into the next room.*

MISSION 4

RESTORE POWER TO THE SHOCK POINT ASSEMBLY

Evidently this shock point assembly is capable of generating enough power to destroy the PROTEAN Hybrid. Keep an eye on the enemy as you move over to the assembly. Dodge its fire and press the appropriate button to activate one of the three points. Do this for the other two to fully power up the shock point assembly.

▶ Try to reach the assembly.

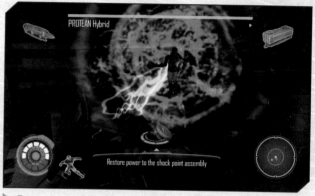

▶ Press the appropriate buttons to power up the assembly.

ACTIVATE THE SHOCK POINT ASSEMBLY

Now that the shock point assembly is fully powered, you must activate it with the PROTEAN Hybrid nearby. The computer that controls the assembly is in the other room. If you just fly over to it, the enemy will follow.

▶ The PROTEAN Hybrid will follow you into the other room.

As before, hit it with everything you have until it starts to regenerate health. This gives you the time needed to dodge into the other room and use the computer. The doors close and the shock point assembly is activated—destroying the PROTEAN Hybrid.

▶ When the PROTEAN Hybrid regenerates its health, dodge into the next room.

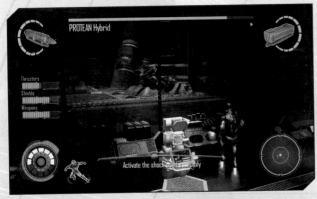

▶ Use the computer before it can exit the room.

▶ The shock point assembly takes care of the enemy for good.

New Achievements

Completing Mission 4 earns you the Anti-PROTEAN Achievement. Plus if you complete it with both Iron Man and War Machine, you get the Man and Machine Achievement.

NEW SUIT AVAILABLE

Completing Mission 4 with at least 436,500 Field Data unlocks the Iron Man Extremis suit.

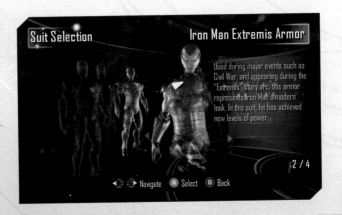

5 OPERATION DAYBREAK

MISSION DESCRIPTION

Back aboard the Helicarrier, as Rhodey recuperates, Tony realizes they were fooled by ULTIMO pretending it's JARVIS. He makes sure that never happens again, and just then, AIM forces attack the Helicarrier. Thinking fast, Tony grabs the suitcase suit and flies into the fight.

PRIMARY OBJECTIVE

Defend the S.H.I.E.L.D. Helicarrier from attacking AIM forces and get Rhodey and the Stark plane out of danger.

MAX FIELD DATA

MISSION	1,170,000
OPPOSITION	71,500
SUIT INTEGRITY	58,500
TOTAL	1,300,000

RECOMMENDED LOADOUT

IRON MAN

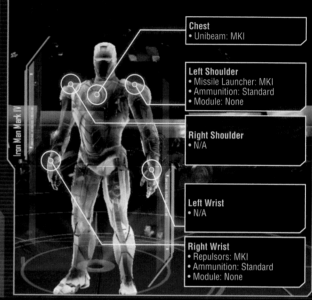

Iron Man Mark IV

Chest
• Unibeam: MKI

Left Shoulder
• Missile Launcher: MKI
• Ammunition: Standard
• Module: None

Right Shoulder
• N/A

Left Wrist
• N/A

Right Wrist
• Repulsors: MKI
• Ammunition: Standard
• Module: None

WAR MACHINE

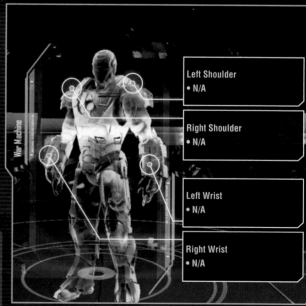

War Machine

Left Shoulder
• N/A

Right Shoulder
• N/A

Left Wrist
• N/A

Right Wrist
• N/A

PROTECT THE HELICARRIER REPULSOR ENGINES (I)

AIM forces attack the Helicarrier and Iron Man is stuck with a very limited suit. You have Repulsors and Missiles available. Initiate flight and head over to the attacking PROTEAN Hybrids.

S.H.I.E.L.D. Helicarrier

Thrusters

Shields

Weapons

Protect the Helicarrier repulsor engines

▶ AIM forces attack the front, starboard side engines first.

KEEP THE ENGINES CLEAR

Throughout this mission PROTEAN Hybrids attack the engines while Grappler Drones, Patrol Drones, and Wasps attack Iron Man. Your main objective is to keep the Hybrids off the engines. If you see one engaged with an engine, focus your attention there.

S.H.I.E.L.D. Helicarrier

Reloading

Protect the Helicarrier repulsor engines

MISSIONS

Quickly launch missiles at the AIM transport, before focusing on the two PROTEAN Hybrids. Hit them with missiles whenever they are available and charge the Repulsors. Keep the Grappler Drones in view if possible or be ready for missile warnings.
Deflect these at the PROTEAN Hybrids to take them out faster.

▶ *Deflect missiles at Hybrids.*

DEALING WITH DRONES

Throughout this mission, Patrol Drones pester Iron Man with their melee attacks. You can take the time to counter and defeat them or you can immediately grapple and reprogram them.

PROTECT THE HELICARRIER REPULSOR ENGINES (2)

Once the first two PROTEAN Hybrids are defeated, three more attack the opposite engine. Take flight, target one, and charge up the Repulsors. Once you are close enough to see its health meter, launch missiles and release the Repulsors.

▶ Deflect the missiles back at the enemy.

▶ Prepare your weapons while flying toward the PROTEAN Hybrids.

MAINTAIN TWO ENGINES

Iron Man needs to keep at least two of the Helicarrier engines operational. If the PROTEAN Hybrids are able to knock out two of the engines, it is game over.

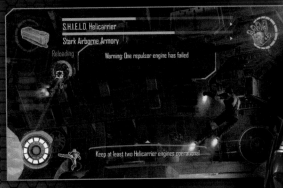

As before, focus your fire on the PROTEAN Hybrids whenever they are attacking an engine. Try to stay on the opposite side as the Grappler Drones so you can see them fire their missiles. At least use the warnings to get ready. Deflect the missiles at the PROTEAN Hybrids.

AIM Wasps join the fight. Get close enough so Iron Man can grab and throw them at another drone. Continue lighting up the PROTEAN Hybrids until they're defeated.

▶ *AIM Wasps join the fight.*

PROTECT THE STARK PLANE

At this point AIM decides to attack Stark's plane. Quickly fly to the jet and intercept the Grappler Drones. Dash from drone to drone—grappling and converting them to your side. Fire on distant enemies as you do so.

▶ *Hit distant enemies with your missiles.*

▶ *Convert the Grappler Drones to your side.*

Continue to reprogram and defeat the rest of the AIM forces that attack the plane, including the pesky Wasps that enter the fight.

PROTECT THE HELICARRIER REPULSOR ENGINES (3)

JARVIS warns Iron Man when a new wave of attackers approaches. Three more PROTEAN Hybrids come after the nearby starboard side engine. Drop off the side of the ship and engage them. Watch out for incoming missiles and deflect them at the Hybrids.

▶ *Take on the three PROTEAN Hybrids.*

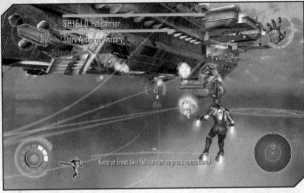

▶ *Deflect missiles back at the enemy.*

PROTECT THE HELICARRIER REPULSOR ENGINES (4)

Once the three PROTEAN Hybrids are eliminated, five more attack the final engine. Immediately take off and target one. As soon as you are close enough, start firing at it.

▶ *Speed over to the PROTEAN Hybrids.*

MISSION 5

Stay focused on the PROTEAN Hybrids because this is the toughest engine to keep intact. Your biggest problem here is the Patrol Drones that harass Iron Man. Hit each of the Hybrids so that they stop firing on the engine, then jam on the Grapple button to reprogram the drones.

▶ *Focus your fire on the PROTEAN Hybrids.*

▶ *Reprogram the Patrol Drones.*

PROTECT THE STARK PLANE

▶ *Fly toward the Stark plane.*

Once the five PROTEAN Hybrids have been eliminated, Rhodey warns that the plane is once again under attack. Quickly fly to the stern of the Helicarrier

Target the PROTEAN Hybrid that hovers above the plane and take it out before concentrating on the Grappler Drones below. When you get close to the Grappler Drones, grapple them and convert them to your side.

▶ *Fire on the Grappler Drones below.*

Patrol Drones are dropped into the fight, so reprogram them with a press of the Grapple button. Continue to eliminate or reprogram the drones until they are no more. At this point the Stark jet is able to take off and Iron Man jumps aboard with AIM Transports in tow.

▶ *Grapple the Patrol Drones.*

▶ *Finish off the drones.*

New Achievements

Completing Mission 5 earns you the Improvisation Under Fire Achievement.

Earn Defensive Player of the Year by saving all four repulsor lifts and all four stabilizers on the Helicarrier.

NEW SUIT AVAILABLE

Completing Mission 5 with at least 1,261,000 Field Data unlocks the Iron Man Mark III suit.

6 WAR MACHINE

MISSION DESCRIPTION

An AIM Arc Armiger is dropped onto the deck of the Helicarrier. Rhodey goes to save the day.

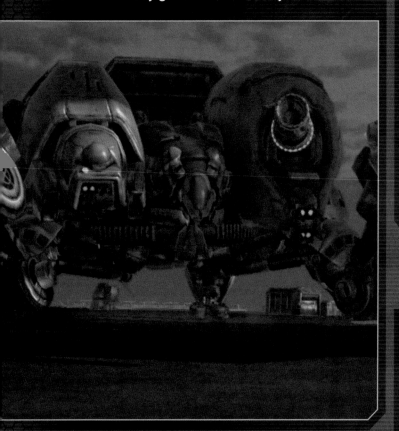

PRIMARY OBJECTIVE

Destroy the AIM "Arc Armiger" battle platform and save the S.H.I.E.L.D. Helicarrier.

MAX FIELD DATA

MISSION	3,348,000
OPPOSITION	204,600
SUIT INTEGRITY	167,400
TOTAL	3,720,000

RECOMMENDED LOADOUT

IRON MAN

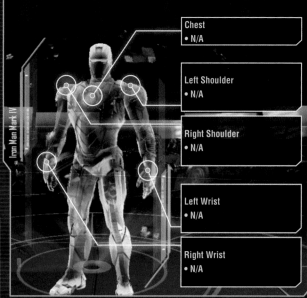

Iron Man Mark IV

Chest
• N/A

Left Shoulder
• N/A

Right Shoulder
• N/A

Left Wrist
• N/A

Right Wrist
• N/A

WAR MACHINE

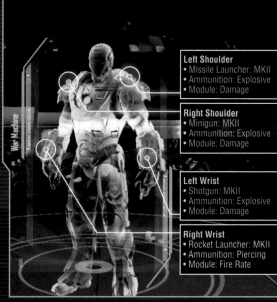

War Machine

Left Shoulder
• Missile Launcher: MKII
• Ammunition: Explosive
• Module: Damage

Right Shoulder
• Minigun: MKII
• Ammunition: Explosive
• Module: Damage

Left Wrist
• Shotgun: MKII
• Ammunition: Explosive
• Module: Damage

Right Wrist
• Rocket Launcher: MKII
• Ammunition: Piercing
• Module: Fire Rate

PROTECT THE HELICARRIER FROM THE AIM ARC ARMIGER

The AIM Arc Armiger is an advanced piece of machinery that takes a great deal of weapon power to shut down. Plus, it has PROTEAN technology giving it the ability to regenerate health.

▶ *The AIM Arc Armiger is an advanced machine.*

Target the nearby Patrol Drones and fly over to them. Take them out before targeting the big Arc Armiger. Two health bars appear at the top of your HUD. The top bar shows the Arc Armiger's health, while the bottom shows the health of the S.H.I.E.L.D. Helicarrier. The objective for this mission is to get the Arc Armiger health bar to empty before the Helicarrier's health depletes completely.

▶ *Take out the two Patrol Drones.*

▶ *Destroy the Arc Armiger before it destroys the Helicarrier.*

Hover above the big enemy while War Machine pumps it full of missiles and rockets. Try to stay focused on the Armiger, but if a Patrol Drone interrupts you, take it out quickly with the shotgun.

Keep the Arc Armiger from destroying the tower.

▶ Take out any annoying drones.

The Arc Armiger stops in front of the tower with the intent of taking it down. Fly over to it and launch everything you have at it. After knocking off a quarter of its health, it starts to heal itself.

▶ Once a quarter of its health is gone, it decides to heal itself.

QUARTER SPLITS

This mission is split into four segments. For every 25% of the Arc Armiger's health that you take away, you reach a checkpoint. If you fail, you can restart at the last checkpoint reached.

Four probes emerge from the Armiger and protect it with lasers. Dodge the lasers and launch a salvo of missiles at the probes. At this point a wave of AIM forces attack the Helicarrier. Try to get a few shots in before changing focus to the little guys.

▶ Hit the probes when they emerge.

TAKE OUT TRANSPORTS

If you see an AIM transport coming, stop what you are doing and take it out before it drops more troops. Doing so can simplify things by reducing the number of enemies you face.

▶ Watch out for the big cannon.

Various drones attack the ship. Take out the Wasps with the Minigun and counter the Patrol Drones, before returning to the Arc Armiger. Watch out when it faces War Machine and fires its laser cannon. Dodge to the side to avoid taking damage.

GOING FOR ACHIEVEMENTS

When the Arc Armiger launches its missiles at War Machine, you have an opportunity to deflect them back. However, in order to earn all achievements, you must defeat the Arc Armiger without using missile deflection. This only needs to be done once, so if you plan on replaying the mission, feel free to use missile deflection here.

More drones attack while the Armiger continues to ravage the tower. Take care of the Wasps with the Minigun and the Patrol Drones with the shotgun. Meanwhile, hit the Arc Armiger with heavy ordnance whenever available.

▶ *Quickly eliminate the drones that attack.*

▶ *Launch the heavy artillery at the Arc Armiger.*

Once the Arc Armiger's health is down to half, it regenerates health again. Dodge the probes and head for the AIM transports that drop off more troops—including Grappler Drones this time.

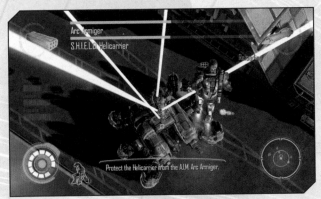

▶ *Dodge the fire from the probes.*

▶ *Take down the AIM transports.*

Keep an eye on the health bars; work to keep the Helicarrier's health bar higher than the Arc Armiger's. Continue to fight off the AIM forces and launch your rockets and missiles at the Arc Armiger.

You reach the final checkpoint as the Arc Armiger reaches 25% health. More troops join the fight at this point. Continue to pound the Arc Armiger while fending off the AIM drones.

▶ *Fight off the AIM forces.*

▶ *The final checkpoint is reached once the Arc Armiger is down to 25% health.*

Keep up the assault on the Arc Armiger until its health bar is depleted and it slumps over. Rhodey and Nick Fury look for a way to finish off the Arc Armiger for good, but Tony Stark has a better idea.

Arc Armiger

S.H.I.E.L.D. Helicarrier

Reloading

Thrusters

Weapons

48m

Protect the Helicarrier from the A.I.M. Arc Armiger.

▶ Continue to attack the Arc Armiger until you deplete its health bar.

New Achievements

Completing Mission 6 earns the Operation Daybreak Achievement. If you defeat the Arc Armiger without using missile deflection, you earn the Brute Force Achievement.

NEW SUIT AVAILABLE

Completing Mission 6 with at least 3,608,400 Field Data unlocks the Classic Iron Man suit.

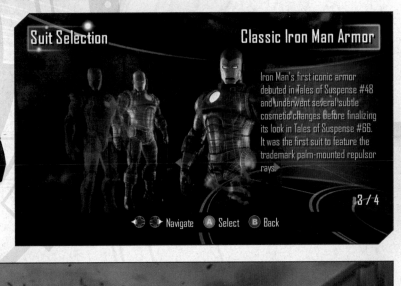

Suit Selection — Classic Iron Man Armor

Iron Man's first iconic armor debuted in Tales of Suspense #48 and underwent several subtle cosmetic changes before finalizing its look in Tales of Suspense #66. It was the first suit to feature the trademark palm-mounted repulsor rays.

3 / 4

Navigate Ⓐ Select Ⓑ Back

MISSION 6

7 STORM WARNINGS

MISSION DESCRIPTION

The AIM Arc Armiger, now rewired by Tony to be an ally, fights alongside the hero as he tears apart a massive power-transmission facility built by AIM using stolen Stark technology: GREENGRID.

PRIMARY OBJECTIVE

Bring some payback to AIM and DeWitt by dismantling the GREENGRID power projector.

MAX FIELD DATA

MISSION	9,558,000
OPPOSITION	584,100
SUIT INTEGRITY	477,900
TOTAL	10,620,000

RECOMMENDED LOADOUT

IRON MAN

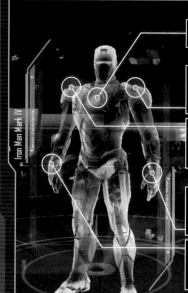

Iron Man Mark IV

Chest
- Unibeam: MKII

Left Shoulder
- Missile Launcher: MKII
- Ammunition: Explosive
- Module: Hybrid

Right Shoulder
- Rocket Launcher: MKII
- Ammunition: Thermite
- Module: Fire Rate

Left Wrist
- Blasters: MKII
- Ammunition: Explosive
- Module: Damage

Right Wrist
- Repulsors: MKIII
- Ammunition: Standard
- Module: Hybrid

WAR MACHINE

War Machine

Left Shoulder
- Missile Launcher: MKII
- Ammunition: Explosive
- Module: Hybrid

Right Shoulder
- Minigun: MKII
- Ammunition: Explosive
- Module: Hybrid

Left Wrist
- Shotgun: MKII
- Ammunition: Explosive
- Module: Damage

Right Wrist
- Rocket Launcher: MKII
- Ammunition: Thermite
- Module: Fire Rate

PROTECT THE "ARC ARMIGER" BATTLE PLATFORM

The Arc Armiger has been rewired to be an ally, but it needs Iron Man or War Machine to protect it. A health bar for the Arc Armiger shows up on the top of your HUD. Don't let this empty or it is game over. Stay just ahead of it so that the AIM forces don't harass it too much.

▶ *Stay close to the front of the Arc Armiger.*

Hold Down on the D-pad to select targets for your ally. The longer you hold it, the more targets are selected. The targeting unit replaces Iron Man's Invincibility or War Machine's Omega System. Use this to select the turrets for the Arc Armiger, while your hero concentrates on the drones. If you don't select its targets, it will select its own targets.

▶ *Mark the turrets for the Arc Armiger.*

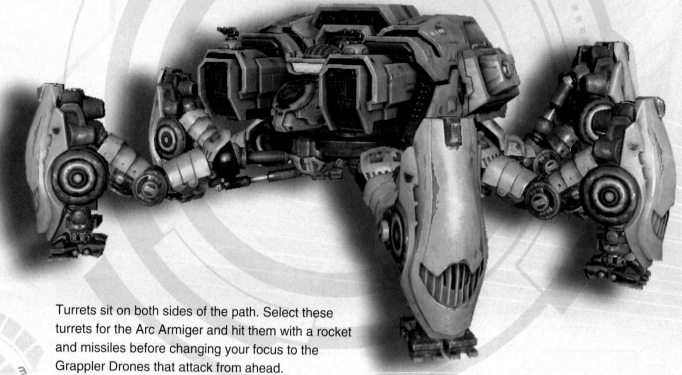

Turrets sit on both sides of the path. Select these turrets for the Arc Armiger and hit them with a rocket and missiles before changing your focus to the Grappler Drones that attack from ahead.

▶ **Have the Arc Armiger take out the turrets.**

Keep the drones off the Arc Armiger. Take them out quickly or they can eat away your ally's health. As

you turn to the left, continue to mark the turrets for the Arc Armiger. Work on the turrets yourself after taking out the drones.

▶ **Keep the drones off the Arc Armiger.**

At this point the Arc Armiger breaks through the gate. A few waves of AIM Wasps fly toward your hero. Take them out with the Repulsor or Minigun before they reach the Armiger.

▶ The Arc Armiger busts through the gate.

▶ Take out the waves of Wasps.

Once you are close enough, select the upcoming turrets as targets for the Arc Armiger. While it takes down the turrets, focus your weapons on the Grappler Drones. If one becomes vulnerable, hijack it and convert it to your side.

▶ Select the turrets as targets for the Arc Armiger.

▶ Take out the Grappler Drones.

▶ If given the chance, hijack a Grappler Drone to fight on your side.

There are several turrets on both sides, so keep the Arc Armiger targeted on them. Let your hero take care of the Grappler Drones. Stay alert for incoming missiles and deflect them back at the enemy. Continue through this area taking out the Grappler Drones and turrets along the way.

MEDIC!

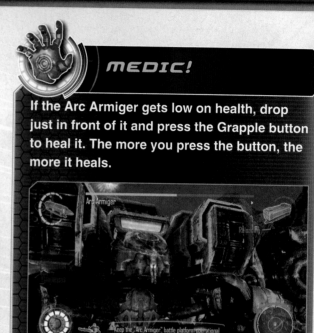

If the Arc Armiger gets low on health, drop just in front of it and press the Grapple button to heal it. The more you press the button, the more it heals.

▶ Deflect missiles back at the enemy.

PROTECT THE "ARC ARMIGER" BATTLE PLATFORM FROM THE ARMIGERS

As the Arc Armiger and the hero enter the next area, they are confronted by four Armigers. Immediately mark one and launch everything you have at it.

▶ Mark an Armiger and hit it with everything.

Keep an eye and ear out for their missiles and deflect them back. This speeds up the fight considerably. Defeat two of the Armigers and your Ally takes care of the rest.

▶ *Deflect its missiles back.*

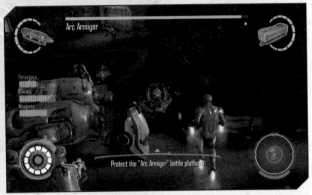

▶ *The Arc Armiger makes quick work of the Armigers.*

PROTECT THE "ARC ARMIGER" BATTLE PLATFORM—INTRODUCING AIM DYNAMOS

Fly just ahead of the Arc Armiger into the next area and mark the turrets for the Arc Armiger before knocking down the Wasps. Once they are out of the way, fly closer to the bridge ahead and start taking out the three turrets on the bridge.

▶ *Knock down the Wasps with the Repulsor.*

▶ *Watch out for the three turrets on the bridge.*

A new wave of Wasps attack as your hero reaches more turrets. Assign the Arc Armiger to attack the turrets while you eliminate the little guys.

At the next bridge, have the Arc Armiger work on the turrets above while your hero fights the AIM forces. This includes your first look at the AIM Dynamos and their Silos. These guys are tough and they are able to launch a cruise missile from their back.

▶ Have the Arc Armiger target the tougher turrets.

▶ Introducing the AIM Dynamos.

▶ The AIM Dynamos are a tough fight.

After your hero and his ally get past the tough Dynamos and turrets, there is a short break. Fly ahead a little and take out the Wasps to the right before turning left to face a row of Dynamos.

▶ Take out the Wasps.

▶ A row of Dynamos is next.

Mark the first Dynamo for the Arc Armiger and start hitting it with missiles from your hero. It launches its missile before coming after your hero. Take it out before marking the next Dynamo.

▶ Take down the first Dynamo.

KEEP ARC ARMIGER SAFE

After you see a Dynamo's missile launched, find it as it comes down. Destroy it before it hits the Arc Armiger.

Three more Dynamos are waiting for their turn. To make it even tougher there are a few turrets and more Wasps to deal with as well. Keep the Arc Armiger focused on the turrets or a Dynamo, while your hero takes out the Wasps and Dynamos.

▶ Keep the Arc Armiger focused on the turrets.

▶ Take out the Wasps between Dynamos.

The bridge bristles with three turrets, and there are more turrets below. Destroy these turrets as you continue into a new area.

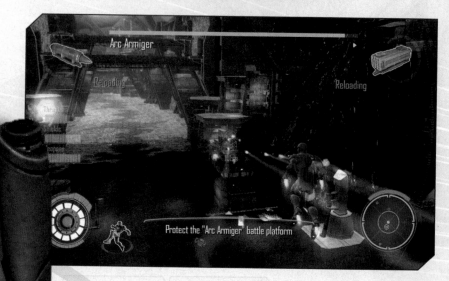

More turrets lie ahead. Stay close to the Arc Armiger, especially if its health is high. Keep it focused on the turrets while your hero eliminates any wandering Wasps.

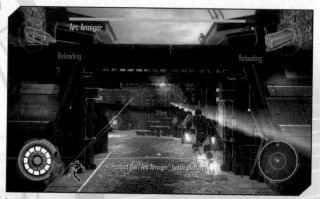

▶ *Stay close to the Arc Armiger while destroying the turrets.*

▶ *Eliminate the pesky Wasps.*

Several more turrets and a few waves of Wasps block the way to your destination. Continue to mark the turrets with Arc Armiger.

▶ Take out the turrets.

DISABLE THE GREENGRID CENTRAL POWER STRUCTURE

With help from the Arc Armiger, your hero reaches the central power structure. Go around the outside of the structure and take out the three turrets.

▶ The Arc Armiger and your hero reach their destination.

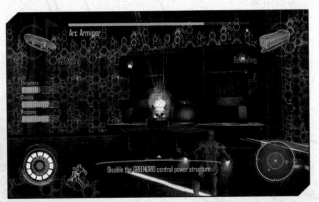

▶ Take out the three turrets around the outside.

Grappler Drones and Wasps continually try to make things more difficult. Keep the Arc Armiger on the turrets while the hero takes down these drones.

Once the three turrets are destroyed, head to the center of the GREENGRID central power structure—an objective marker shows the location. Get within 100 meters so that you see its health meter and launch a rocket at the power structure.

MISSION 7

Wasps and Grappler Drones try to make things more difficult.

Mark the central power structure.

REPOSITION THE GREENGRID RELAYS

You must reposition the three relays that are now marked on your radar. A timer starts to count down from 45 seconds. Guide your hero to the nearest one and press the indicated button to start the repositioning. Fill up the meter by continually pressing the same button. Once it is done, quickly fly to the next relay.

Reposition the relays.

Quickly fly between the relays.

Once the timer reaches zero, the relays go back in the ground. Any relays that have been repositioned remain, so disable the power structure again and finish the remaining relays. To get all three relays in one run, fly between them and immediately jam on the button when close. Once they are in place the GREENGRID power projector is destroyed and the mission is complete.

▶ *You must be quick to get all three relays in one run.*

New Achievements

The goal is to get all three relays repositioned without being interrupted by an enemy attack. This earns you the Switchboard Operator Achievement.

Completing Mission 7 earns you the Stormbreaker Achievement. Plus if you complete it with both Iron Man and War Machine, you get the Bipolar Achievement.

If you complete this mission without repairing the Arc Armiger, you earn the Guardian Achievement.

NEW SUIT AVAILABLE

Completing Mission 7 with at least 10,301,400 Field Data unlocks the Silver Centurion suit.

8 ULTIMO

MISSION DESCRIPTION

After shutting down the power-transmission facility, our heroes go to face down the 600-foot battle chassis that was receiving all that power: ULTIMO. Iron Man fights DeWitt inside the colossus, while War Machine takes apart the monster from the outside.

PRIMARY OBJECTIVE

Defeat the ULTIMO doomsday machine and stop DeWitt once and for all.

MAX FIELD DATA

MISSION	27,324,000
OPPOSITION	1,669,800
SUIT INTEGRITY	1,366,200
TOTAL	30,360,000

RECOMMENDED LOADOUT

IRON MAN

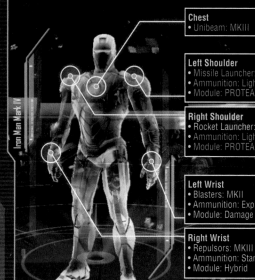

Iron Man Mark IV

Chest
• Unibeam: MKIII

Left Shoulder
• Missile Launcher: MKII
• Ammunition: Lightning
• Module: PROTEAN

Right Shoulder
• Rocket Launcher: MKII
• Ammunition: Lightning
• Module: PROTEAN

Left Wrist
• Blasters: MKII
• Ammunition: Explosive
• Module: Damage

Right Wrist
• Repulsors: MKIII
• Ammunition: Standard
• Module: Hybrid

WAR MACHINE

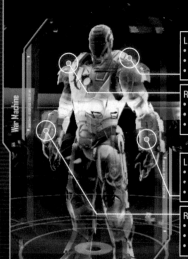

War Machine

Left Shoulder
• Missile Launcher: MKIII
• Ammunition: Lightning
• Module: PROTEAN

Right Shoulder
• Minigun: MKII
• Ammunition: Standard
• Module: Hybrid

Left Wrist
• Shotgun: MKII
• Ammunition: Standard
• Module: None

Right Wrist
• Rocket Launcher: MKII
• Ammunition: Lightning
• Module: PROTEAN

WAR MACHINE — DEFEAT ULTIMO

Now that the GREENGRID power facility has been destroyed, Iron Man and War Machine can go after ULTIMO and DeWitt—with some help from S.H.I.E.L.D. forces. Iron Man slips inside ULTIMO to see what makes it tick while War Machine stays outside and deals with the 600-foot behemoth.

▶ *War Machine takes on ULTIMO.*

DOUBLE TEAM

Iron Man and War Machine are needed for this mission, so have them both ready before you start.

War Machine is up first. There are eight arc reactors that are exposed on the outside of ULTIMO's chassis—five on its front and three down the spine. War Machine must take these out to limit its power.

▶ *Eight arc reactors are exposed on Ultimo.*

When ULTIMO lifts his hand, he launches a salvo of missiles at War Machine. Target one of the front arc reactors and deflect the missiles toward that reactor while you continue to move forward. ULTIMO hunches over, providing an opportunity to move in close.

Watch out when you get close to ULTIMO. It reaches back with its right appendage and swings at War Machine, knocking him down to the ground. If War Machine is knocked down, rapidly press the indicated button to recover and shoot the bottom of its foot.

▶ Deflect its missiles at one of the arc reactors.

▶ ULTIMO hunches over.

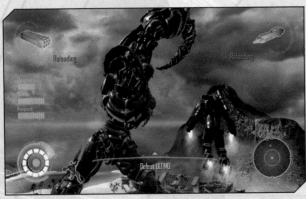

▶ ULTIMO swings at War Machine.

▶ Recover quickly to avoid foot stomp.

It has a few other attacks that you must watch for. When it looks directly at War Machine and opens its mouth, it releases a breath-type attack. It doesn't hurt War Machine too much—only taking away a small part of his shield. This attack can hit War Machine no matter what side of its head he is on.

▶ Ultimo's breath attack.

▶ Avoid its eyebeam attack.

It also has an eyebeam attack that fires two laser beams from its eyes. It sweeps slowly from one side to the other. This is easily avoided by dashing above or below the beams. Quickly fly above or below the beams and fire on one of the reactors or use this opportunity to rip out a reactor (if it's possible).

Continue to counter his attacks with some shots to the arc reactors. Once one becomes vulnerable, indicated with an icon that resembles a button on your controller, fly in close and use that button to rip out the arc reactor. Remove two of these reactors and the scene changes to Iron Man inside ULTIMO.

▶ *Hit a reactor until it becomes vulnerable.*

▶ *Remove two vulnerable arc reactors.*

IRON MAN — DEFEAT ULTIMO

Iron Man discovered DeWitt inside his personal PROTEAN Hybrid suit. DeWitt detaches himself from ULTIMO so that he can fight off Iron Man. Armored cabling is still attached to his back and he uses it effectively.

▶ *DeWitt detaches from ULTIMO.*

DeWitt uses some melee attacks on Iron Man, but his most devastating move is the spin attack. As he spins toward Iron Man, the armored cabling whips everything in his path causing big damage.

DeWitt's Hybrid attacks Iron man.

Watch out for spin attack.

Stay a safe distance from him and continuously fire rockets and missiles. Keep dashing in the opposite direction, while eroding his health.

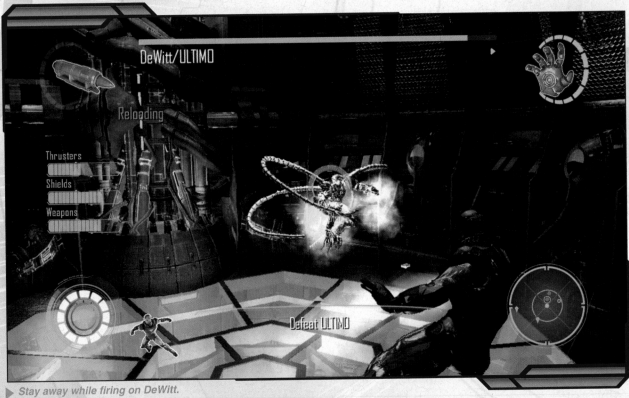

Stay away while firing on DeWitt.

MISSION 8

IRON MAN — DEFEAT ULTIMO'S DEFENSIVE TURRETS

Once you knock off a quarter of his health, DeWitt releases three defensive turrets. Stay on the move to avoid their fire and pound them with some of your own. The turrets are more vulnerable when open, so hit them hard with the Repulsor at this time. Take out the three turrets and the scene shifts back to War Machine.

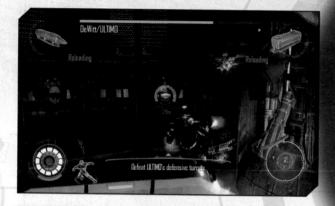

WAR MACHINE — DEFEAT ULTIMO

War Machine receives a message from Nick Fury that they are capable of launching the "Perfect Storm" at ULTIMO. This is actually ULTIMO who has taken this move and now has the ability to use it on War Machine.

▶ *Nick Fury launches "Perfect Storm."*

Besides this new ability, ULTIMO has the same attacks as before. As before deflect its missiles at the arc reactors or work in close and take them out with your own arsenal.

▶ *Wear down the arc reactors.*

Take out another of the front reactors before flying behind its head to work on the rear arc reactors. If you can stay behind ULTIMO, these rear reactors can be easier to reach. Remove four more reactors to weaken him enough so that Iron Man can finish off DeWitt.

IRON MAN — DEFEAT ULTIMO

Use the same strategy as before. Stay away from DeWitt's Hybrid while blasting him with some heavy weaponry. Don't get in the way of his spin attack.

▶ *Remove four more vulnerable reactors.*

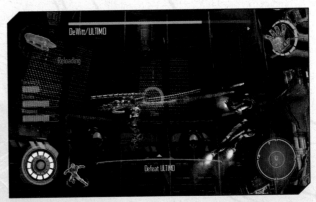

▶ *Watch out for devastating spin attack.*

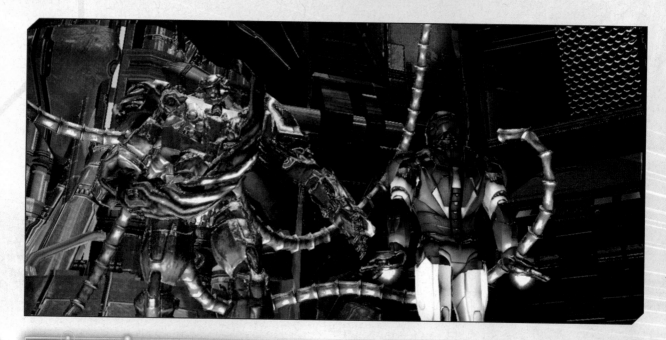

MISSION 8

IRON MAN — DEFEAT ULTIMO'S DEFENSIVE TURRETS

Remove enough health and he releases three more defensive turrets. Eliminate these while staying on the move to avoid their fire.

▶ Eliminate the defensive turrets.

IRON MAN — DEFEAT ULTIMO

Focus on DeWitt and continue to maintain a good distance between him and Iron Man. Fire everything you have at him to take him down.

WAR MACHINE — TAKE THE SHOT

DeWitt's Hybrid grabs Iron Man. Now Iron Man must use every ounce of his energy to finish him, but needs some quick help from War Machine.

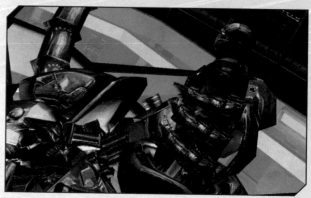

▶ DeWitt gets a hold of Iron Man.

A timer appears that counts down from 45 seconds. War Machine must focus all his power at ULTIMO's head. Immediately target the head and fire missiles and rockets. Switch to the Minigun and shotgun to deplete its health. Now it is up to S.H.I.E.L.D. to use their Helicarrier to finish the behemoth.

► War Machine has 45 seconds to take out ULTIMO's head.

► Finish off ULTIMO.

New Achievements

If Iron Man and War Machine did not take any damage, you earn the Not a Scratch Achievement. This refers to the suit's armor integrity not the shielding. So as long as your shield can regenerate, you can get this achievement.

Complete Mission 8 to receive the Bigger They Are Achievement. You also receive one

to three of the complete game achievements depending on what difficulty was played. Any easier difficulties are earned too. If you played on Normal Difficulty, you also get the Ultimatum Achievement for completing Easy Difficulty.

NEW SUIT AVAILABLE

Completing Mission 8 with at least 29,449,200 Field Data unlocks the Ultimate Iron Man suit. If you have unlocked all of the suits to this point, you also receive the Hall of Armors Achievement.

UNLOCKABLE ARMOR

As you complete the missions in *Iron Man 2* you unlock new suits for Iron Man. These suits are purely cosmetic. Everything operates the same no matter what suit is selected.

IRON MAN

IRON MAN MARK I   unlocked by completing mission 3 with 155,200 field data

This first-ever Iron Man suit was built during the character's initial appearance in Tales of Suspense #39, and this design originates from the interpretation from Iron Man Vol. 4 #5.

IRON MAN MARK II   unlocked by completing mission 2 with 48,500 field data

Tony constructed the Iron Man Mark II to explore flight potential. It was later converted into the War Machine armor.

IRON MAN MARK III unlocked by completing mission 5 with 1,261,000 field data

The Mark III suit is Tony's first "full-featured" suit, and is the first with Iron Man's signature red and gold color scheme.

UNLOCKABLE ARMOR

IRON MAN MARK IV
unlocked from beginning

The Mark IV suit is superior to the Mark III in areas such as suit weight, comfort, and ease of assembly. Tony built it to replace the Mark III after that suit was damaged in the fight with Obadiah Stane.

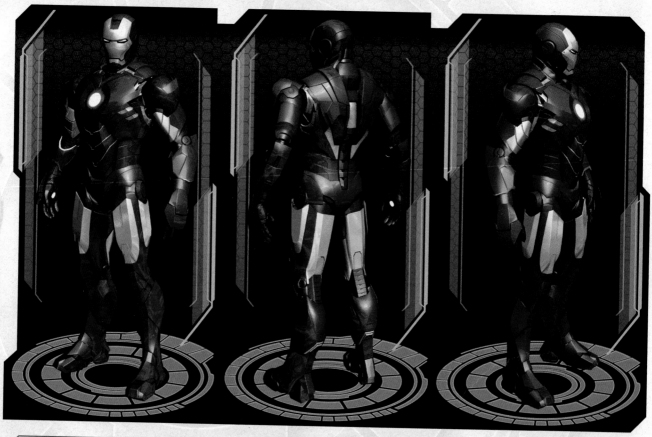

IRON MAN MARK V

The Mark V suit is the "Suitcase Suit" that appears only during Mission 5. It lacks many of the features available in the other Iron Man armor suits, but its portability is an enormous asset for Tony Stark.

The mark VI suit is an advanced variant of the Mark IV, adapted to match improvements to the reactor technology in Tony's chest. It also contains special upgrades to combat new threats Tony encountered since creating the Mark IV.

UNLOCKABLE ARMOR

IRON MAN EXTREMIS ARMOR unlocked by completing mission 4 with 436,500 field data

Used during major events such as Civil War, and appearing during the "Extremis" story arc, this armor represents Iron Man's modern look. In this suit, he has achieved new levels of power.

CLASSIC IRON MAN ARMOR unlocked by completing mission 6 with 3,608,400 field data

Iron Man's first iconic armor debuted in Tales of Suspense #48 and underwent several subtle cosmetic changes before finalizing its look in Tales of Suspense #66. It was the first suit to feature the trademark palm-mounted repulsor rays.

UNLOCKABLE ARMOR

SILVER CENTURION ARMOR
unlocked by completing mission 7 with 10,301,400 field data

Sporting new colors, Tony used this suit during his fight with Iron Monger, his days as a West Coast Avenger, and in the first "Armor Wars" storyline.

ULTIMATE IRON MAN
unlocked by completing mission 8 with 29,449,200 field data

In the Ultimate Universe, an alternate version of the Marvel Universe, Tony Stark requires the help of an entire specialized crew to help maintain this bulkier Iron Man armor.

WAR MACHINE
unlocked from beginning

Piloted by James Rhodes, War Machine was created when Hammer Industries and the U.S. military added weaponry and armor to an existing Iron Man Mark II platform. It is highly durable and carries substantial conventional firepower.

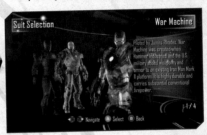

UNLOCKABLE ARMOR

There are 11 mission specific accomplishments that are earned by doing something well during the missions. These are explained further within the walkthrough. Otherwise, complete the game on the highest difficulty and defeat many enemies with each weapon to earn most of the rest of the Achievements and Trophies.

PLAY THROUGH

This group of Achievements and Trophies are obtained by playing through the eight missions.

NAME	DESCRIPTION	MISSION	POINTS
Shake It Off	Recover from the Roxxon EMP attack.	1	3
Access Denied	Prevent Roxxon from stealing the Stark Archives.	1	10
Deportation	Prevent the Russian separatists from deploying Roxxon Armigers.	2	15
Power Outage	Defeat the Crimson Dynamo.	3	15
Anti-PROTEAN	Destroy Project PROTEAN.	4	20
Improvisation Under Fire	Save Rhodey and the Stark mobile armory from the A.I.M. attack.	5	20
Operation Daybreak	Defeat A.I.M. and save the S.H.I.E.L.D. Helicarrier.	6	20
Stormbreaker	Shut down the GREENGRID power transmitter.	7	20
The Bigger They Are	Defeat Ultimo.	8	30

MISSION SPECIFIC ACCOMPLISHMENTS

The following Achievements and Trophies are earned by doing something well throughout the missions. The following table tells which mission each is earned. More information about each is included in the walkthrough of this guide.

NAME	DESCRIPTION	MISSION	POINTS
Not In My House	Prevent the first wave of Roxxon dropships from deploying their drones.	1	15
Full Flight	Only one S.H.I.E.L.D. transport lost in the canyon run.	2	15
Area Secured	At least 10 S.H.I.E.L.D units survive the battle for the docks.	2	20
Pulling The Plug	Destroy all four Tesla reactor stabilizers in under 60 seconds.	3	15
Anger Management	Destroy most of the structures in Shatalov's base.	3	15
Entrapment	Reach the bottom of the elevator shaft without touching a laser tripline.	4	15
Defensive Player Of The Year	Save all four repulsor lifts and all four stabilizers on the S.H.I.E.L.D. Helicarrier.	5	20
Guardian	Shut down GREENGRID without needing to repair the Arc Armiger.	7	25
Switchboard Operator	Reposition all of the GREENGRID relays without being interrupted.	7	20
Not A Scratch	Defeat ULTIMO with no armor damage.	8	40

GAME COMPLETION

Three of these Achievements and Trophies are earned by completing the game on each of the three difficulties. You earn the achievement that corresponds to the difficulty completed plus any easier difficulties. Therefore these three can be completed all at once by just playing on the Formidable Difficulty.

Technical Genius is earned by inventing everything in Research. This requires 62,671,000 Field Data.

NAME	DESCRIPTION	POINTS
Ultimatum	Complete every mission on Easy difficulty.	15
Iron Man	Complete every mission on Normal difficulty.	30
Invincible	Complete every mission on Formidable difficulty.	100
Technical Genius	Invent every module, ammunition, and weapon upgrade.	50

DEFEAT ENEMIES

The following Achievements and Trophies are earned by defeating a certain number of enemies with specific weapons or with each hero's special ability. Mission 2 has a number of enemies that are easily defeated after upgrading. The docks of Mission 2 provide a good opportunity to get Unnecessary Force—earned by defeating a soldier with Unibeam. Bulletproof and Omega Man are good incentives to use the special abilities whenever available. Keep track of which ones you have earned, then switch up the weapons that you use most often. Don't forget about Iron Man's Laser, which isn't equipped by default.

NAME	DESCRIPTION	POINTS
Fists Of Iron	Defeat 100 enemies in close combat.	20
Storm Of Lead	Defeat 100 enemies with War Machine's minigun.	20
Fire And Forget	Defeat 100 enemies with homing missiles.	10
Subtle Like A Rocket	Defeat 100 enemies with the rocket launcher.	15
Room Broom	Defeat 100 enemies with War Machine's shotgun.	20
Extra Crispy	Defeat 100 enemies with Iron Man's laser.	20
Pushback	Defeat 100 enemies with Iron Man's repulsor.	20
Up Close And Personal	Defeat 100 enemies with Iron Man's blaster.	20
Overkill	Defeat 100 enemies with Iron Man's unibeam.	25
Gonna Need Some More Bad Guys	Defeat more than 1,000 enemies.	30
Unnecessary Force	Defeat a soldier with Iron Man's unibeam.	7
Bulletproof	Defeat 50 enemies in melee as Iron Man while Invincible.	30
Omega Man	Defeat 100 enemies as War Machine while using the Omega System.	30

THE SUITS

All of Iron Man's suits are earned by completing each mission with the necessary amount of Field Data. The following table shows which mission the suit is earned in and how much field data is needed.

NAME	DESCRIPTION	MISSION	FIELD DATA	POINTS
Mark VI	Unlock the Mark VI Iron Man armor.	1	21,600	10
Mark II	Unlock the Mark II Iron Man armor.	2	48,500	10
Classic Mark I	Unlock the Classic Mark I Iron Man armor.	3	155,200	10
Extremis	Unlock the Extremis Iron Man armor.	4	436,500	10
Mark III	Unlock the Mark III Iron Man armor.	5	1,261,000	10
Classic Iron Man	Unlock the Classic Iron Man armor.	6	3,608,400	10
Silver Centurion	Unlock the Silver Centurion armor.	7	10,301,400	10
Ultimate Iron Man	Unlock the Ultimate Iron Man armor.	8	29,449,200	10
Hall Of Armors	Unlock all armor suits.	All	N/A	35

BOTH HEROES

For four missions, you earn an extra achievement for completing the mission with both Iron Man and War Machine. These missions are 2, 3, 4, and 7.

NAME	DESCRIPTION	MISSION	POINTS
Two Man Army	Defeat the Russian Separatists as both Iron Man and War Machine.	2	10
It Takes Two to Tangle	Defeat Crimson Dynamo as both Iron Man and War Machine.	3	10
Man and Machine	Defeat Project PROTEAN as both Iron Man and War Machine.	4	10
Bipolar	Shut down the GREENGRID power transmitter as both Iron Man and War Machine.	7	10

PLATINUM TROPHY

NAME	DESCRIPTION	MISSION	POINTS
Unlock all trophies.	Earn all Iron Man 2 trophies.	N/A	N/A

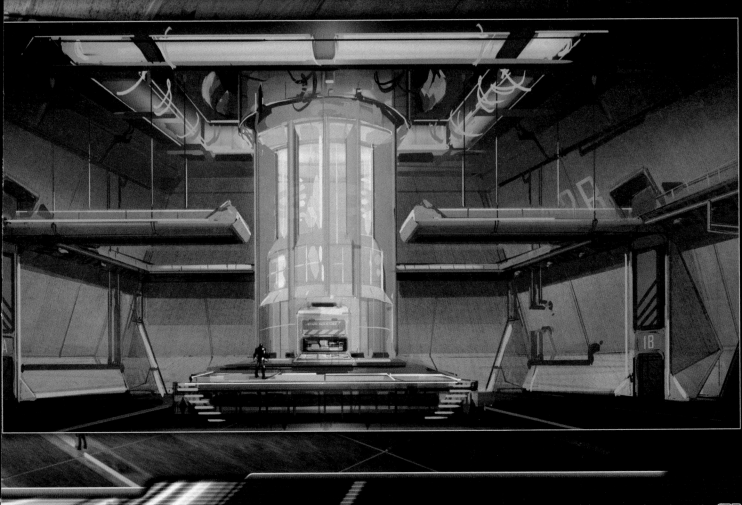

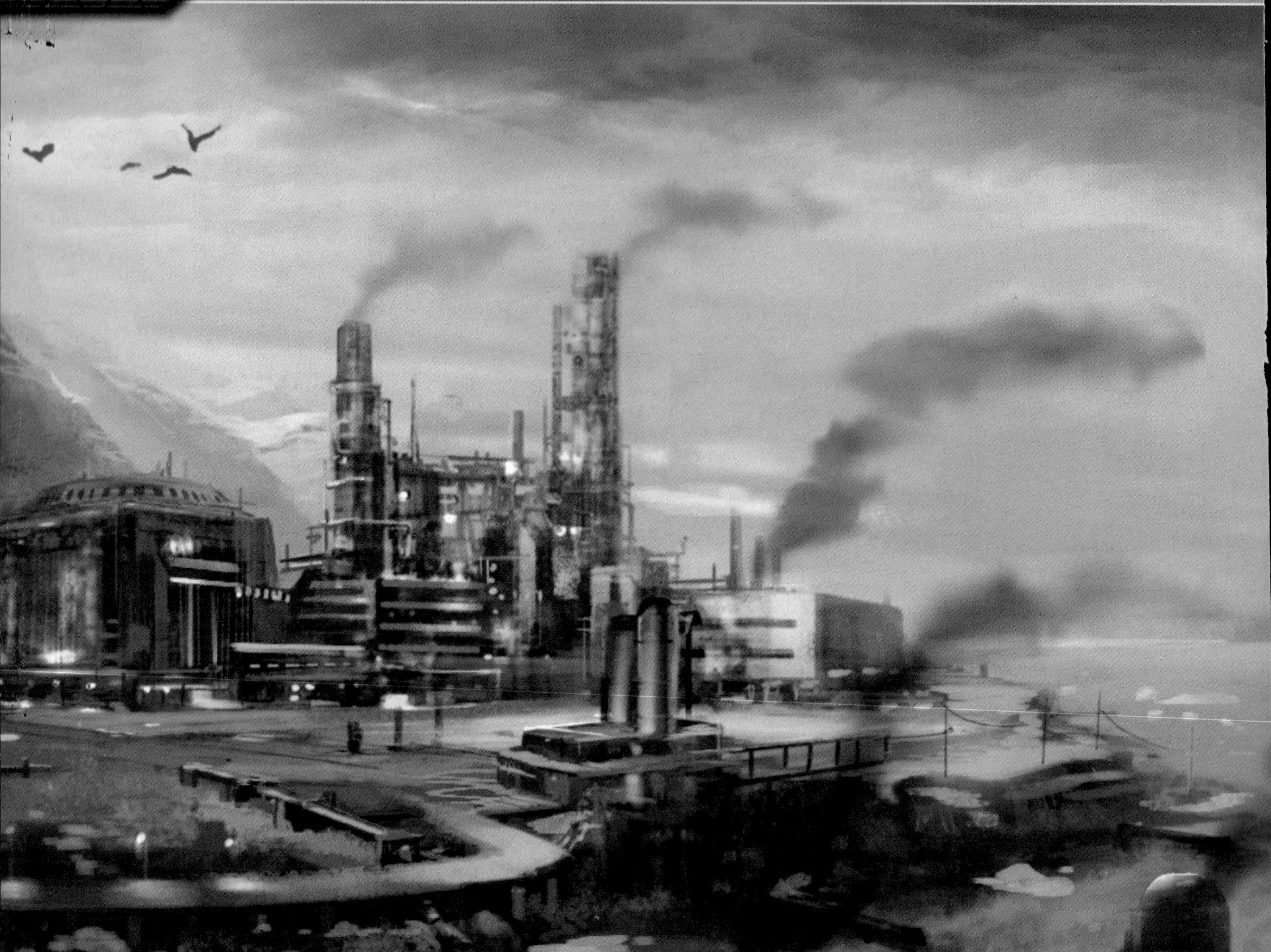

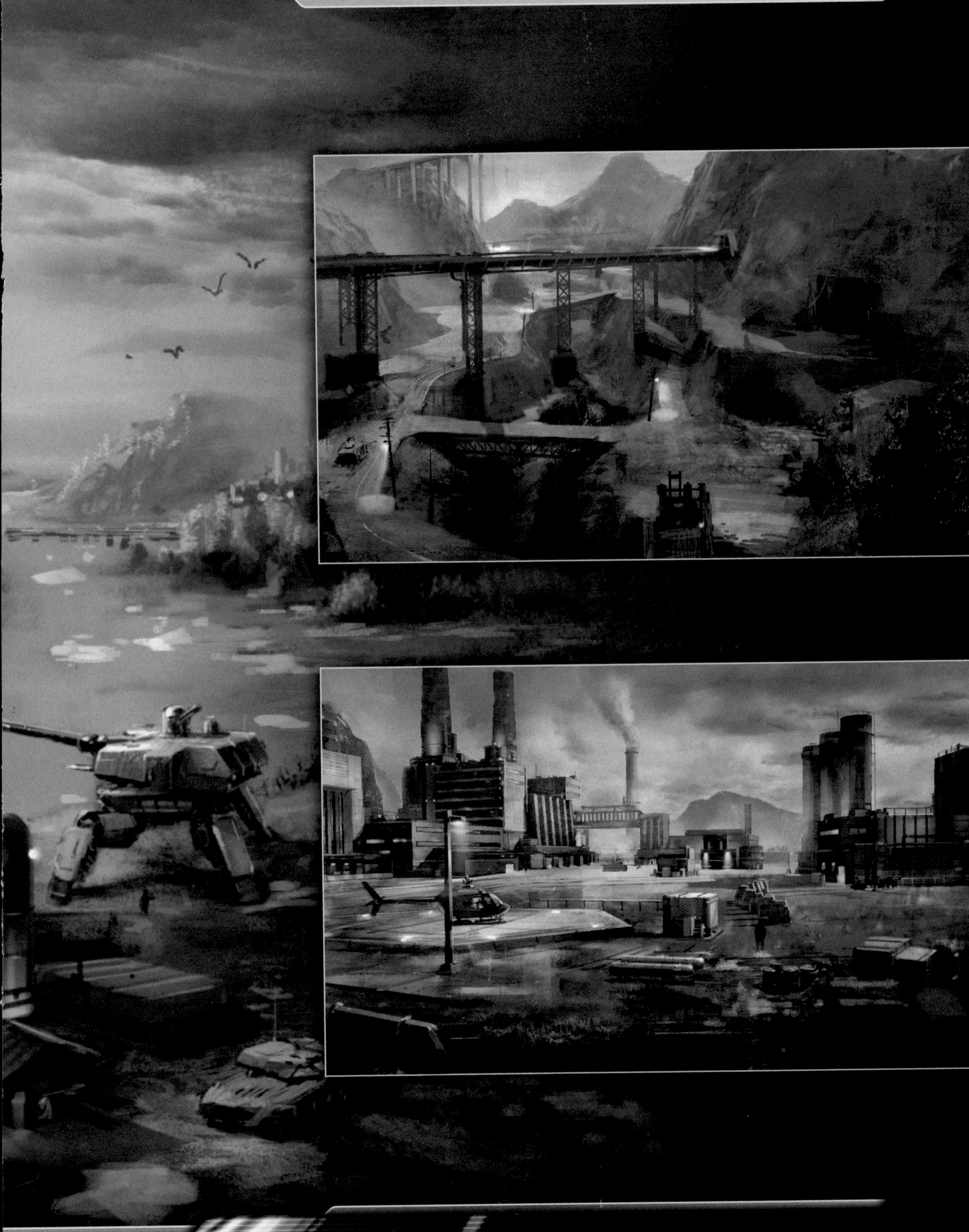

S.H.I.E.L.D.

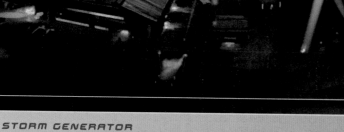

STORM GENERATOR

IRON MAN & CRIMSON DYNAMO

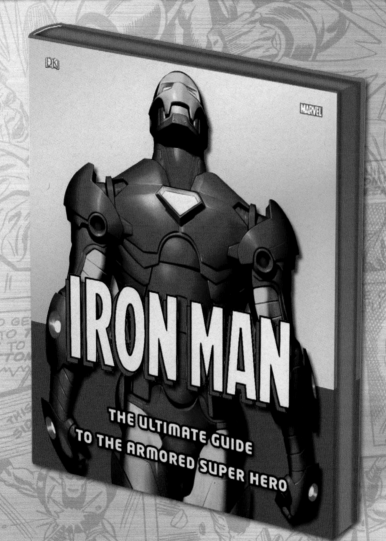

MARVEL STUDIOS

IRON MAN 2

OFFICIAL STRATEGY GUIDE

Written by Michael Owen

DK/BRADYGAMES, A DIVISION OF PENGUIN GROUP (USA) INC.
800 East 96th Street, 3rd Floor
Indianapolis, IN 46240

ISBN-10: 0-7440-1205-8

ISBN-13: 978-0-7440-1205-7

Printing Code: The rightmost double-digit number is the year
of the book's printing; the rightmost single-digit number is the
number of the book's printing. For example, 10-1 shows that the
first printing of the book occurred in 2010.

13   12   11   10   4   3   2   1

Printed in the USA.

BRADYGAMES STAFF

Publisher
David Waybright

Editor-In-Chief
H. Leigh Davis

Licensing Director
Mike Degler

International Translations
Brian Saliba

CREDITS

Senior
Development Editor
Ken Schmidt

Book Designer
Dan Caparo

Production Designer
Tracy Wehmeyer